INT

City, MI

OF CABBAGES AND KINGS

Of Cabbages and Kings™
1991

THE YEAR'S BEST MAGAZINE WRITINGS FOR KIDS

Selected by Kimberly Olson Fakih

R. R. BOWKER
New Providence, New Jersey

Published by R. R. Bowker,
a division of Reed Publishing (U S A) Inc.

Printed and bound in the United States of America

International Standard Book Number 0-8352-3072-4
International Standard Serial Number 0000-1376

Grateful acknowledgment is made to the magazines and other copyright owners, listed below, for permission to reprint their materials. All possible care has been taken to trace ownership and secure permission for each selection. If, in some instances, this has proved impossible, or if any have been inadvertently overlooked, we will be pleased to make the necessary arrangements at the first opportunity.

"Hurray for Hedgehogs!" from the March–April 1990 issue of *International Wildlife*. Reprinted by permission. Copyright ©1990 by the National Wildlife Federation. Photograph of hedgehog with flower copyright © Hans Reinhard/Bruce Coleman Ltd.; hedgehog in terracotta pot copyright © George McCarthy/Bruce Coleman Ltd.

"The Tale before Peter Rabbit" from the January–February 1990 issue of *International Wildlife*. Reprinted by permission. Copyright © 1990 by the National Wildlife Federation. Illustrations p. 11 from *The Tale of Peter Rabbit* by Beatrix Potter, copyright © Frederick Warne & Co., 1902, 1987; reproduction of front cover, from the first Warne paper-covered boards edition of *The Tale of Peter Rabbit*, courtesy Frederick Warne & Co.; illustration by Beatrix
(*continued on page 235*)

ISBN 0-8352-3072-4
9 780835 230728

CONTENTS

ACKNOWLEDGMENTS

A single volume of the Better Homes and Gardens anthologies for young readers was a well-worn bedside companion in my childhood—through it I met Christina Rossetti, Edward Burgess, the Goops, the Pickwicks and many others whose names did not sink in although their works, or the works they appeared in, did. It never failed me: there was a limited number of selections but like a cold crock of sweet butter that is never empty, there was always more to read—even if I'd read it before with less avid interest. Certainly I never thought about the authors, artists, or others who had worked to make the book real, but truly, an anthology requires the kindness of strangers as few books do. I would be a Goop if I did not thank them all.

To those people who promised help and delivered it, a debt is owed: to Sarah Hale, at *Cobblestone*, for many gentle phone calls as well as quick and thorough aid; to Mary Ann Hocking and Ron McCutchan at *Cricket*, who separately worked through myriad details, it seems, namely in the spirit of cooperation; to the people at the National Geographic Society who look just as good behind the scenes as the magazine they produce; and to John Boslough, Jere Van Dyk, and Michael Yamashita for their generous allowances in the use of their material for a special readership. Also thanks to Angela Szablewski of Bowker, for her help with the paperwork; and to countless others who individually tracked down authors, artists, and photographers for me that I might secure permission to use their works. Thank you.

Gratitude to Dorothy M., always a friend. And finally, to someone who was a stranger but is one no longer, many thanks: Marion Sader, who first approached me with the idea for this book, and whose energy and unwavering enthusiasm helped carry the project from a mere inception into an inevitable reality.

INTRODUCTION

Question: How do you read this book?

Answer: Any way you want.

There is no plot that clutters *this* book, nor are there lists of characters to remember—although there are heroes to cheer for and villains to despise. There aren't any clues, and you (finicky browser, window-shopper, runaway reader) don't need to start at the beginning. You may just open it up to any page, and see if you like the article or story there. If not, it is understood, you'll find another page. Even though this book has an order not of your choosing, you won't need to worry about that. You probably will not want to read everything in one sitting. And you don't have to.

This collection of the best stories and articles to have appeared in magazines for children over the period of a year (September 1989–August 1990) is different from other books. It doesn't set you on a course and keep you there, suspended and mesmerized, from start to finish. Unlike other reading materials—like a single-story book—which absorb you completely in their tales over a stretch of time, both anthologies and magazines require a different reading habit: they depend on your flipping back and forth, playing with the ideas, day-dreaming, lost in reverie for an entire afternoon, or at separate time periods. *You* decide when and what you want to read, or glance at, or muse over. This book, like a machinery of words and pictures of many parts and fragments, requires you, the reader, as the ghost of the machine to work and move and "run." In fact, you don't have to actually read at all. Leaf through it. Look. Pictures, photographs, games. Ignore one article. Read another. Flip past the part you might read later on. Skip other selections completely. It's a peculiar—and rewarding—aspect of anthologies, though: the very pieces you aren't interested in this time around might be the ones you read first next time. No matter—you're in charge of what you read. If you don't like one story, lump it—then kindly suit yourself with another selection. Blaze your own trail through these pages, and make them your own.

Before you start, however, you may heed a word or two about what can be called coherence, or structure, or categories. There *happen* to be some captivating articles included that, if seized by someone out to teach you a lesson or two, would be neatly summed up under chapter headings such as "Geography" or "Science" or "Sports." It seemed more important, somehow, to let you know, among other information, which way is up (Chapter 3) rather than instruction about, say, "Space, Directionality, and Geography"; or about craft and craftiness (Chapter 5) rather than heavy talk about "History, or Civilization, or High Culture"; who's in charge (Chapter 6) instead of big words like "Tradition, or Psychology, or Discipline, or Politics"; what to expect when you're among the woodland folk (Chapter 4) or why the Golden Rule is key to gardening, but not to starlings (Chapter 7) in place of such thick topics as "Social Behavior and Belief Systems."

The variety reflected in these choices gives you, as simply as possible, a hint of the wide-ranging, appealing ideas found in magazines for children. Each of them has a distinct identity. And the only thing these magazines usually have in common is that they are interested in entertaining *you*. Some of these magazines have unifying themes in each issue; while these are excellent magazines, that structure—of putting all the articles in this anthology under one big umbrella—just wouldn't be a fair representation of what is being published for you.

So you come up with your own themes. If you've ever watched fireworks, you know that they can look, at first, like a lot of random explosions. But then you realize that there are patterns in the lights, and clusters of explosions, accompanied by booms, hisses, and whistles. It all depends on what kind of fuel you use, and when you ignite it. Get it?

Lastly, a word about gender and age group. There's something here for everyone. When you're older, you'll read "men's" magazines or "women's" magazines—you probably flip through them now. But with the exception of the title of *Boys' Life* (and not necessarily its content), the magazines for children attempt to strike a clear balance in stories and articles of interest to both boys and girls. So does this anthology.

Kimberly Olson Fakih
JANUARY 1991

OF CABBAGES AND KINGS

1

IN SEARCH OF THE HEDGEHOG

How to track a hedgehog's nighttime wanderings? Just attach a spool of thread to its back and let it go. It will make its own trail. Where to take an injured hedgehog? St. Tiggywinkle's hospital. No kidding—these people take hedgehogs very seriously, and want to make sure the prickly little characters are around for a long time to come. So give a cheer:

Hurray for Hedgehogs!

By David M. Schwartz

Pity the poor hedgehog: Baked in mud and eaten by gypsies, pursued by medieval medicine men (who used its various body parts to cure baldness, blindness, boils and stones) and slaughtered by farmers who believed it suckled cow's milk—the prickly little European mammal has been persecuted for centuries. Today, it frequently drowns in ponds, disappears into storm drains, gets entangled in netting, mown down with the grass, burned up with autumn leaves and, most conspicuously, squashed on country roads. Making matters worse, its habitat is shrinking.

Envy the lucky hedgehog: Blessed with a friendly, beseeching face and an endearing character, the spiny nocturnal creature thrives in suburban areas right alongside people. In Great Britain, this accessibility has given rise to a nationwide infatuation and spawned lively commerce in clothing, toys, trinkets, figurines, stationery and "hedgehogabilia" of every sort. An expanding legion of two-legged fans also provides the creature with food, rescues it from deep abysses and even delivers the injured to St. Tiggywinkle's, the special hedgehog care unit of a wildlife hospital.

It is, in fact, the best of times and the worst of times for the European hedgehog. And nowhere is the simultaneous contrast in fortunes more evident than in Britain, where scientists have begun to unravel the mysteries and marvels of hedgehog life in the shadow of people.

Found throughout the European continent, *Erinaceus europaeus* is one of about a dozen members of the hedgehog family, a group of insect-eating mammals that populate only the Old World. By hedgehog standards, the European species is mid-sized—8 to 12 inches long and weighing 1 to 2 pounds. Known more for its spines than its speed, *E. europaeus* does exhibit its own kind of grace as it appears to glide through the grass on hidden legs. When threatened, it neither fights nor flees but erects its spines, tucks in its soft underparts and humps itself up. A drawstring-like dermal muscle turns its body into an impenetrable ball. So spherical are curled-up hedgehogs that Lewis Carroll's fictional Alice used them to play croquet.

"It seems that practically everyone in this country has a soft spot in his heart for hedgehogs," says Pat Morris, a mammalogist who has studied the animals for more than 20 years. He is not immune himself. On Morris's desk at the University of London's Royal Holloway and Bedford New College sits a plastic hedgehog pen-and-pencil holder; it grips writing implements between its spines, and has an eraser as a nose and a pencil sharpener at the other end.

"They are among the most appreciated native species, and one of the most instantly recognized," says Morris. "Yet their familiarity has bred no great scientific interest over the years, partly because they have no real economic or medical significance." Hedgehogs do not destroy crops, prey on poultry or spread serious disease. Come dusk, they simply put their heads to the ground and wander about, letting their sensitive noses lead them on an erratic path through pastures, hedges, lawns and yards in search of slugs, caterpillars and other small animals.

With no proprietary interests in real estate, hedgehogs are among the handful of mammals that are completely unterritorial. During the breeding season, males simply extend their nightly peregrinations, increasing their chances of bumping into a female. When one happens by, he circles her, snorting loudly and rhythmically until she flattens her spines and allows him to approach. ("How do hedgehogs mate?" asks an old riddle. "*Very carefully.*")

The general indifference of hedgehogs toward each other makes life difficult for scientists such as Pat Morris who are trying to estimate their populations. Because the animals travel alone and in darkness, often in bushes and tall grass. they are nearly impossible to count. By trapping and fitting hedgehogs with radio transmitters, biologists have found that the size of their home ranges varies considerably—from fewer than one to more than 100 acres—and that the travel routes of several hedgehogs may overlap. "So we have a fairly common, familiar mammal but no accurate way of determining its population density or overall population, and no way to know for certain whether it is increasing or decreasing," says Morris.

Just the same, he is reasonably certain there are fewer hedgehogs around today than 50 years ago, although the thorny insectivores were probably more common at that time than they were 10,000 years earlier, before Britain's forests were cleared for agriculture. Up until a few decades ago, most British farms produced an assortment of crops and livestock in patchworks of small fields divided by woody hedgerows. Pasture land and hedges (for which the animal is named) provide it with ideal nesting habitat and an abundance of small invertebrate prey.

But European agriculture has undergone a massive face lift since World War II. Fields have been enlarged to accommodate modern equipment, and hundreds of thousands of miles of hedgerow have been dug up. Where sheep and cattle once grazed, wheat and barley now grow in an endless continuum of fields broken only by the occasional barbed-wire fence. Farmers improve their yields by spraying insecticides and molluskicides which further diminish the hedgehog's food supply.

In 1986, Martin Dowie, a graduate student of Morris, wanted to see how the animals were faring in a part of Hampshire where agriculture has been extensively modernized. "I set 70 traps every night for three periods of three weeks each," says the 26-year-old Irish-born zoologist, who was smitten with hedgehogs as a child, "and I didn't catch a single one."

Giving up on Hampshire, he moved north to a section of Oxfordshire where farms are smaller and their practices more traditional. In no time he had trapped 11 animals. He fitted each of them with a radio transmitter, and on their backs he glued a small glass container housing a spool of colored thread. As the hedgehogs moved, they left behind a trail of thread. Using portable radio receivers, Dowie and four assistants spent about a fortnight fixing each animal's location at frequent intervals and mapping the thread trails. This way, he was able to see exactly where they had traveled throughout the night.

Ultimately, Dowie hopes to identify the microhabitats ideal for hedgehogs at different times of year, information that may some day help assess the status of hedgehog populations in a given area. "Once we know where hedgehogs *should* be," he says, "we can find out if they actually are there, and if not, we can ask, 'Why not, and what should we do about it?'"

Though his research is not yet complete, it is clear that hedgehogs are scarce in many regions where they once thrived. "The 'hogs do a lot better where farms have plenty of

hedgerow and pasture land, and in areas of human habitation like villages, the fringes of cities and suburbs," says Dowie. Meanwhile, in Germany, biologist Joachim Esser also found that loss of habitat in some rural areas had concentrated the hedgehogs into towns.

It is too early to tell whether the suburban sprawl of the 1980s compensates the animals for their loss of farmland habitat since the '40s. But in many respects, the suburbs are hedgehog heaven. "Residential gardens [yards] have fragmented habitats," explains Pat Morris. "There are trees whose leaves fall to the ground and can be used in nests, places to hide under buildings and shrubbery and a huge plant-species diversity in a small area, so there's likely to be plenty of food."

But most Britons do not need to wait for scientists to confirm that hedgehogs have discovered their neighborhoods, for they have already discovered the hedgehogs. The animals' penchant for residential areas has brought them in close contact with millions of people. In turn, many an English family has adopted the kind of paternalistic attitude toward the creatures that is usually reserved for pets.

Every night from spring until late fall, thousands of bowls of dog food, bread and milk (though milk is not recommended) are set outside to accommodate hedgehogs. Tales abound of hedgehogs scratching at the back door when the bowl is empty, even coming into the kitchen through the cat flap. Yet most of the night wanderers do not reciprocate human kindness with any degree of loyalty.

Pat Morris's radio-tracking studies have shown that most hedgehogs follow variable paths, crossing and recrossing each other's routes in slow but steady meanderings of one-half to two-and-a-half miles per night. Come morning, they find the nearest crawl space or patch of dense shrubbery and hole up for the day. Over the course of a summer, a hedgehog may visit many different day nests—much to the disappointment of human families trying to attract one to call their own. One retired West London couple fed eleven different animals but never managed to get themselves a resident 'hog.

"People get indignant when I say they can't be sure the hedgehog that visits their food bowl is the same from night to night," says Morris. "In one case, by marking the animals, we found 19 different visitors to one house. The people who were feeding them religiously for years thought they were just one!"

Although hedgehogs fascinate him, Morris is puzzled by their enormous popularity. After all, they lack most of the traits that usually make animals appealing. A survey conducted by biologist-author Desmond Morris (no relation to Pat) in the mid-1960s determined that the most popular species are cuddly and round, with big eyes and short, snubbed noses—"all the things that are the exact opposite of hedgehogs!" exclaims Pat Morris. "On top of that," he adds, "hedgehogs have fleas and they're smelly."

Morris's theory is that humans have an inherent desire to reciprocate trusting behavior, and hedgehogs, protected by their spines, can afford to be trusting. Unlike foxes, badgers or other backyard visitors, they do not dig holes or overturn garbage cans, and they may even pay their rent by eating slugs and other garden pests.

But not even their spiky shields can protect them from the variety of difficulties they face in their new status as suburbanites. "Directly or indirectly, all their problems are caused by people," says Steve Micklewright of Avon Wildlife Trust, a nonprofit group in Bristol. "Granted, hedgehogs are a bit careless, but that's part of their charm. It's a terrible shame that their bumbling nature sometimes turns out to be a death sentence."

Putting up for the day in thick, tall grass, hedgehogs are vulnerable to the whirling blades of power mowers. Nesting or hibernating in garden refuse, they can be sent up in smoke during autumn cleanup. Homeowners who keep their yards immaculate weed out potential habitat, while those who put out poisonous "slug pellets" deprive hedgehogs of a favored prey and expose them to toxins. Also, the animals' stiff spines get hopelessly entangled in netting left carelessly on the ground and sometimes make it hard for them to extricate their snouts from discarded food cans.

Although a hedgehog's olfaction is keen,

its vision is poor, and the night prowlers have a way of falling into drains, ditches and freshly dug cellar holes. Small plastic-lined garden ponds, popular all over Britain, are hedgehog death traps: though capable swimmers, the animals can't climb out and they soon die of exhaustion. Livestock barriers called cattle grids—a series of bars across a hole in the road—present another serious pitfall.

But automobile traffic is undoubtedly the greatest peril. Curling into a ball and erecting sharp spines may foil a fox or a badger, but it won't deter the tires of an onrushing car. About 100,000 hedgehogs are squashed every year in Great Britain alone, with a similar carnage reported in many other European countries.

Mindful of so many hedgehog hazards, the British are rising to the challenge of protecting the accident-prone creatures. The Avon Wildlife Trust heavily publicizes its telephone "Hogline," which receives thousands of calls reporting sightings of hedgehogs, living and otherwise. Steve Micklewright, the project's director, says the group is using a computer to map locations of road casualties to see if some sites pose a particular hedgehog hazard.

Hedgehogs also enjoy the ministrations of the British Hedgehog Preservation Society, which raises funds by selling "hedgehogabilia," such as a car window decal featuring a perky hedgehog over the caption "Don't Squash Me!" The Society's mission: educating the public to safeguard hedgehog happiness.

At St. Tiggywinkle's (named after the hedgehog washerwoman in a Beatrix Potter story), Les and Sue Stocker are sorry to report that business is booming. At any given time, 100 to 150 prickly patients—most of them road casualties—are likely to be found in the erstwhile garage that serves as the hedgehog unit of the wildlife hospital the Stockers have set up in their home and yard in Aylesbury, about 50 miles northwest of London. With the help of a veterinarian and volunteer assistants, the Stockers minister to hedgehogs with every imaginable ailment and injury, from fleas and mange to broken bones, sliced snouts and worse. "It can be depressing at times," says Les, "but we've been able to return thousands to the wild since we opened in 1978."

To help keep their spirits up, the Sockers assign each of their charges a nickname appropriate to its condition: "Pegleg," for instance, hops around with one hind leg in a cast, while "Tripod," an amputee, makes do with just three legs; "Curly" has malformed spines. For $17 (U.S.) a year, citizens can help fund the Stockers' Wildlife Hospital Trust by joining their "Adopt a Hedgehog" program.

Although the unfortunate ends that befall huge numbers of hedgehogs upset many people, no one knows exactly what impact the slaughter has on the hedgehogs' population. "They're not particularly rare," says Pat Morris, "and they've been getting flattened on our roads for years. So maybe the fact that we still see so many hedgehogs despite all the road deaths tells us that their populations are quite healthy."

Joachim Esser's study in Germany, however, raises gloomier possibilities. He suggests that, like island faunas, hedgehogs isolated in small village populations are highly vulnerable to catastrophe. The annual road mortalities he observed—as high as five per kilometer—might be enough to drive the animals to extinction in many areas.

Either way, it is clear that what's good for the hedgehog is good for many other wild animals and plants. "Hedgehogs are a flagship for conservation," explains Martin Dowie. The amber light of morning has put an end to a night of hedgehog tracking and revealed the delicate web of red, yellow and green threads spun out over the countryside during the creatures' nighttime wanderings. "People find them cute and humorous, so eventually they ask, 'What do they eat? Perhaps I shouldn't put out slug pellets.' They they say, 'Where do they hibernate? Should I leave a pile of twigs under the garage?'"

Dowie recognizes, however, that hedgehog fanciers, not just scientists, play a vital role in a pursuit that goes beyond the success of just one species. "For most, it starts out as an interest in hedgehogs," he says. "But before long, they've become actively involved in conservation. That's the important thing. Hedgehogs are just a foot in the door."

2

STALKING THE WILD

Hedgehogs were familiar enough to Mrs. Tiggywinkle's friend Beatrix Potter, who was no meek young woman dreaming up bunny tales; she observed not only domestic animals and other fuzzy types, but nature's other creatures—bats, lizards. Her naturalist's approach to this "wild-life" menagerie, as well as plant life, was ignored by the "experts" of the times.

The Tale before Peter Rabbit

By Robert McCracken Peck

When the postman called at the Edwin Moore house in London one September day in 1893, he carried a letter, from family friend Beatrix Potter, addressed to young Noel, sick in bed. "My dear Noel," it began. "I don't know what to write to you, so I shall tell you a story about four little rabbits whose names were—Flopsy, Mopsy, Cotton-tail and Peter. They lived with their mother in a sand bank under the root of a big fir tree."

So enthralling was the story that followed, and so beguiling the sketches accompanying the text, that its recipient carefully put it away to read again and again. Seven years later, Potter asked her young friend if she could borrow back the letter, and within a few months, just before Christmas 1901, *The Tale of Peter Rabbit* first appeared in print. The endearing story of a mischievous young rabbit in a forbidden British garden may well be the most popular children's story of all time.

But there is more to the tale of Beatrix Potter. Before her success with imaginary animals came her extraordinary talent as a wildlife artist and illustrator. Had she been born a man or in another century, she might have found a career in natural history. In the repressive Victorian Era, however, women of her social class were not taken seriously as thinkers, nor were they encouraged to engage in any professional activity. Overlooked, ignored or cruelly rejected by the scientific establishment of her day, Potter gave up her renderings of nature in favor of more acceptable anthropomorphic creatures.

Only in recent years have Potter's talents as a naturalist begun to receive the recognition they deserve. London's Tate Gallery featured her scientific illustrations in an exhibition two years ago, and a book by scholar Anne Stevenson Hobbs published this past fall includes many of Potter's renderings never published before.

The only daughter of a strict upper middle-class family, Beatrix was raised by nannies and tutors in virtual isolation from the outside world. Unlike her younger brother Bertram, who was sent to boarding school, Beatrix never went to school (for which, characteristically, she later said she was grateful, claiming, "It would have rubbed off some of the originality"). She was permitted few friends and no sports.

About the only place in London Beatrix was permitted to venture alone, even as a young woman, was the British Museum of Natural History, whose vast collections lay just blocks from the Potters' proper but cheerless town house. There, amid the grandeur of the dinosaurs, she escaped the prisonlike confines of her third-floor room. Her only prolonged respites came during the family's extended holidays in Scotland and England's Lake District. Whether in the museum or the countryside (where she later settled), Beatrix found nature synonymous with freedom.

With some basic art training from her governess and encouragement from Victorian portraitist and family friend Sir John Everett Millais, Beatrix drew all the natural curiosities she could find—including occupants of her own domestic zoo. There were shells, fossils, flowers, bats, water newts, even a hedgehog. Her favorites were her rabbits, from Benjamin Bouncer to Peter, and she immortalized their antics with pen and brush.

"I cannot rest," she wrote in her secretly coded diary. "I must draw, however poor the result." And draw she did. Her pencil sketches and delicate watercolor studies range from the microscopic scales of a butterfly's wing to the sun-dappled leaves and

Pet lizard Judy, a menagerie member, in 1884. "I have had a great deal of pleasure from that little Creature," Beatrix wrote after Judy died.

This study is thought to be of an actual rabbit named Peter, one of Potter's pets during her late twenties.

Rabbits were not the only animals whose ears fascinated Beatrix. She sketched this long-eared bat with folded wings in 1885, at age 19.

blossoms of a water lily in an English country pond.

In the 1890s, when she was in her mid-twenties, Potter turned her attention to the wild mushrooms and fungi she found during family holidays in Scotland. Whether the appeal was their strange shapes and colors or the excuse to take her pony cart into the countryside alone, they inspired some of her finest painting. Perhaps most important, they brought her into contact with an unlikely and rare source of encouragement, a retired postman named Charlie McIntosh.

McIntosh was an expert on the mosses, ferns and fungi of Perthshire. Described by Beatrix as a "learned but extremely shy man" (not unlike herself), he provided just the outside contact and validation the young artist needed. "He was certainly pleased with my drawings," she wrote, "and his judgement, speaking to their accuracy in minute botanical points, gave me infinitely more pleasure than that of critics who assume more, and know less, than poor Charlie."

Potter's interest in mushrooms and fungi grew to a passion, resulting in more than 300 watercolors that combine scientific accuracy with her own artistic flair. "I have been drawing funguses very hard," she wrote to a friend in 1897. "I think some day they will be put in a book."

At about this time Potter received a further boost from a well-connected uncle, Sir Henry Roscoe, who, in a "sudden fit of kindness," introduced her to authorities at the Royal Botanical Gardens at Kew. But despite her uncle's support and an impressive display of her paintings, the artist was snubbed as a young and inexperienced wo-

Potter painted a watercolor of a boar fish after finding the "strange little red fish" on an 1895 outing on the beach in Weymouth.

For an 1895 study of fly agaric fungi, beech leaves, polypody fern, mosses and lichen, Potter combined elements from different habitats.

man whose place it was to listen and learn, not to instruct others. As disappointed as she must have been, the experience apparently convinced her she knew at least as much as the so-called authorities. She anonymously submitted a scientific paper on the sporing of molds to the prestigious Linnean Society of London and was vindicated when it was accepted.

While her fungus pictures would not be published for another 70 years (in 1967, 59 of her watercolors illustrated *Wayside and Woodland Fungi* by W.P.K. Findlay), the spore of the idea of publishing her paintings had been sown. And if the adult world was going to be so obstinate, why not turn to the audience that seemed to appreciate her most?

For years, Potter had been entertaining children with her menagerie of tame and wild pets and an imagination made fertile by three decades of self-entertainment. In her late twenties, she retrieved her Peter Rabbit letter from young Noel Moore and inserted bits to expand the story. She copied the illustrations, adding some and dropping others, to create a 42-page prototype—only to be rejected by a succession of publishers. Undaunted, Potter published the book herself. The first edition of 250 copies was so popular that she had another 200 printed within a few months. Encouraged by her unexpected success, she resubmitted her book to a leading publisher and was accepted. The book has been in print ever since.

Potter never seemed to regret her shift from fact to fiction. Perhaps for her there was little difference. Peter was, after all, her "affectionate companion and quiet friend" for almost a decade. Her other animal characters were equally "real," often with the physical traits of family pets and the personalities of human acquaintances. (She published her last four books in the United States in part to avoid offending her Lake District neighbors, so recognizable were some of her characters.) Even her settings were based more on fact than fiction. In the paths and parlors of her make-believe world are details of the Cumbrian farm and village she eventually made her home.

Certainly, her diary tells us, she found great satisfaction in every art form she tried. "It is all the same," she wrote, "drawing, painting, modelling." But even if she didn't suffer from her switch to fancy, perhaps the rest of us have. We'll never know what she would have achieved if she had been encouraged to fulfill her "irresistible desire to copy any beautiful object which strikes the eye."

3

KNOWING WHICH WAY IS UP

Figuring out where you're going is an artform, but it's also a sport, called "orienteering." The scouts in this article learned the sport in their troops, but many schools and recreation centers offer courses as well. It may be nice to know that no matter how bad your sense of direction, you'll never be lost again!

Ready . . . Set . . . Go!

By Jon C. Halter

Competitors charge over hills and rush through dells, hurrying to be the first to the finish.

A footrace? Yes—and more. Each competitor carries a compass and a topographic map. This is *orienteering*—the sport in which you run, read a map and compass, and think on your feet.

Orienteering is for individuals or teams. A course can cover many square miles or a few acres.

For your troop's orienteering program feature, you will practice map and compass skills at weekly meetings. Then comes the highlight: an Outback Weekend, filled with direction-finding games and competitions.

You can try one or more of the following types of orienteering.

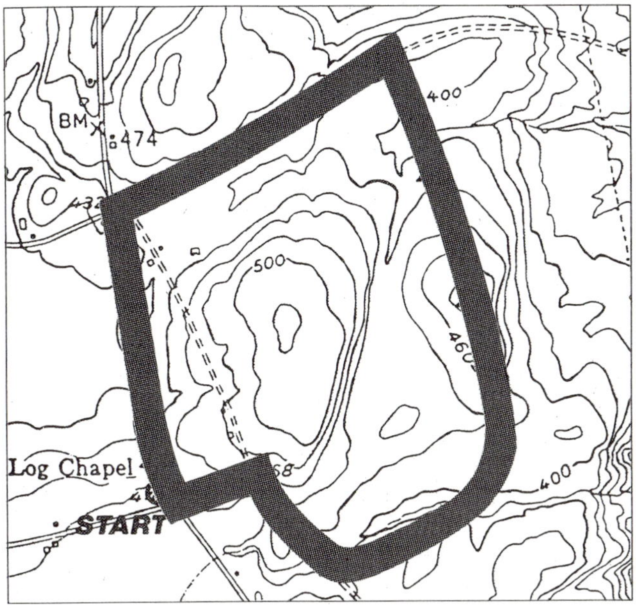

Line Orienteering: Locate the control points on the trail.

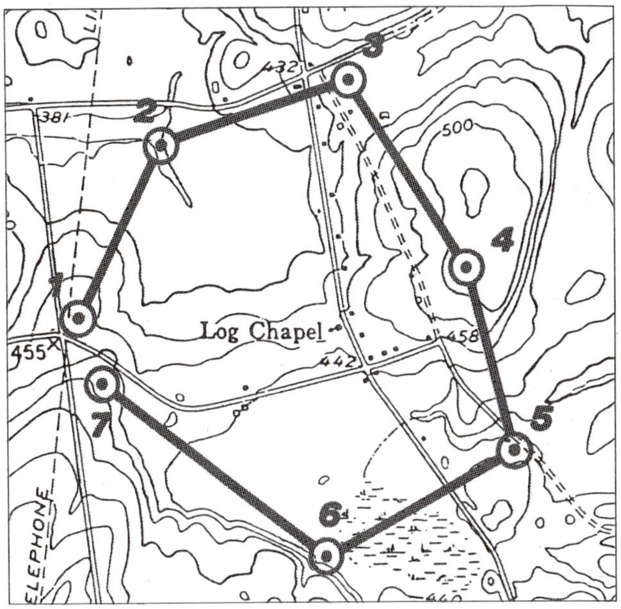

Cross-Country: You pick the best route between all control points.

Line Orienteering. At the start, you copy the official route from a master map onto your own map. As you proceed along the trail, you note on your map the location of any control points (marked by a red-and-white flag). The winner has the most control points correctly positioned.

Route Orienteering. You accompany an adult leader along a route that's not marked on your map. Every so often the group stops and each Scout marks the trail on his own map. The winner is the Scout with the fewest mistakes on his map's route.

Project Orienteering. You need to know camping skills as well as map and compass skills for this. At each control point, you have to perform a test, like cutting a tent peg or decoding a message. You'll get points for each test plus a score for locating the control points on your map.

Cross-Country, or Free, Orienteering. The master map only shows control point location and order. You have to pick the fastest route to each of them, in order. You face tough decisions: Is it faster to go over the hill to the next control point or should you go around? Should you cross the bridge or climb through the dry creek bed? The winner completes the course in the shortest time.

Relay Orienteering. Taking turns, each team member completes a separate loop course out from base camp. Each must reach the three or four controls in his loop and return before the next team member can start.

Score Orienteering. In this race against time, you decide *how* to reach each control and *in what order.* That's because the controls are worth different point totals. You may ask yourself, for example, should I struggle to the toughest location and get 100 points—or bypass it to reach two easier controls worth 50 and 40 points each?

The Scout earning the most points within the time limit is the troup orienteering champion.

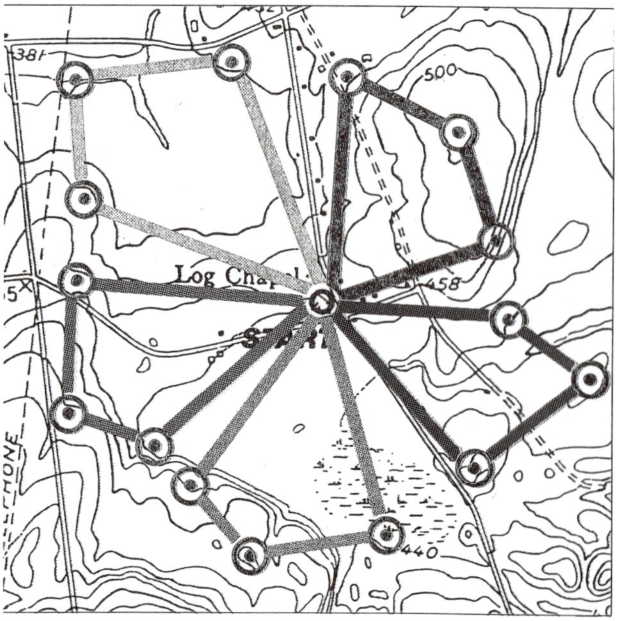

Relay Orienteering: Each team member completes a single loop.

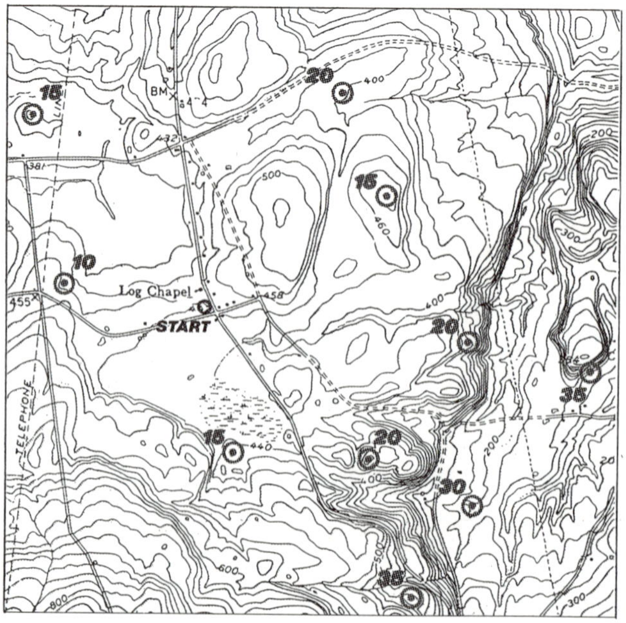

Score Orienteering: You earn points in a race against time.

When the folks at the National Geographic Society tell you it's important to learn how to read a map, take heed. Since 1890, the Society has sponsored 3,700 explorations. Can you imagine how many maps they've gone through?

Start Early, Keep at It, to Learn Map Reading

Once we learn the conventions of map reading, they seem so simple: Up is north, blue is water, a star denotes a capital. But when and how do we learn to read a map?

Research shows that even three-year-olds can master, at least in a basic way, the key map-reading concept: A map is a two-dimensional symbol for three-dimensional space. Linda Acredolo of the University of California, Davis, showed a child a map of a room, pointed out on it where a toy was hidden, and asked the child to find that toy. Depending on the map's orientation, about half the three-year-olds and almost all the five-year-olds could successfully do so.

Three years may be the age at which the idea sinks in. Judy DeLoache of the University of Illinois let children watch her hide a small toy in a scale model of a room and asked them to find a larger version in a real room. "A three-year-old can do it, but a $2\frac{1}{2}$-year-old has no idea that the model has to do with anything larger," she says.

But even if the basic notion is there early, Lynn Liben and Roger Downs of Pennsylvania State University found that children still have a lot to learn. Second graders assume that north is always at the top of a map because of the hanging maps they have seen. "If you ask them to close their eyes and point in the direction of north, often they'll point straight up," says Liben. She says children acquire map-reading skills gradually, and teachers must begin by using maps of familiar areas: their own classrooms, homes, and neighborhoods.

If you've read the article on orienteering, you may think of this as just another version of "Ready . . . Set . . . Go!" from Scienceland. *The difference is that rabbits don't really need to learn which way is up to know precisely where they are headed—they have a very strong and precise sense of direction called Whicheverway! As long as it's* away *from danger!*

How a Rabbit Runs

Each bound of most rabbits covers 2–3 m (7–10 ft). Also, rabbits tire more quickly than hares.

Blazing a trail and battling snowdrifts is a snap with a map, and the right pair of snowshoes. Snowshoes are easy to use, and you can rent them until you know which kind you'd like to buy—those of ash wood with rawhide lacings, or of aluminum with synthetic bindings. You can read more about this brand of traversing the wilderness in "Try Snowshoeing" by Laura Daily in the December 1989 Boys' Life.

Try Snowshoeing

Illustration by Steve Chalker

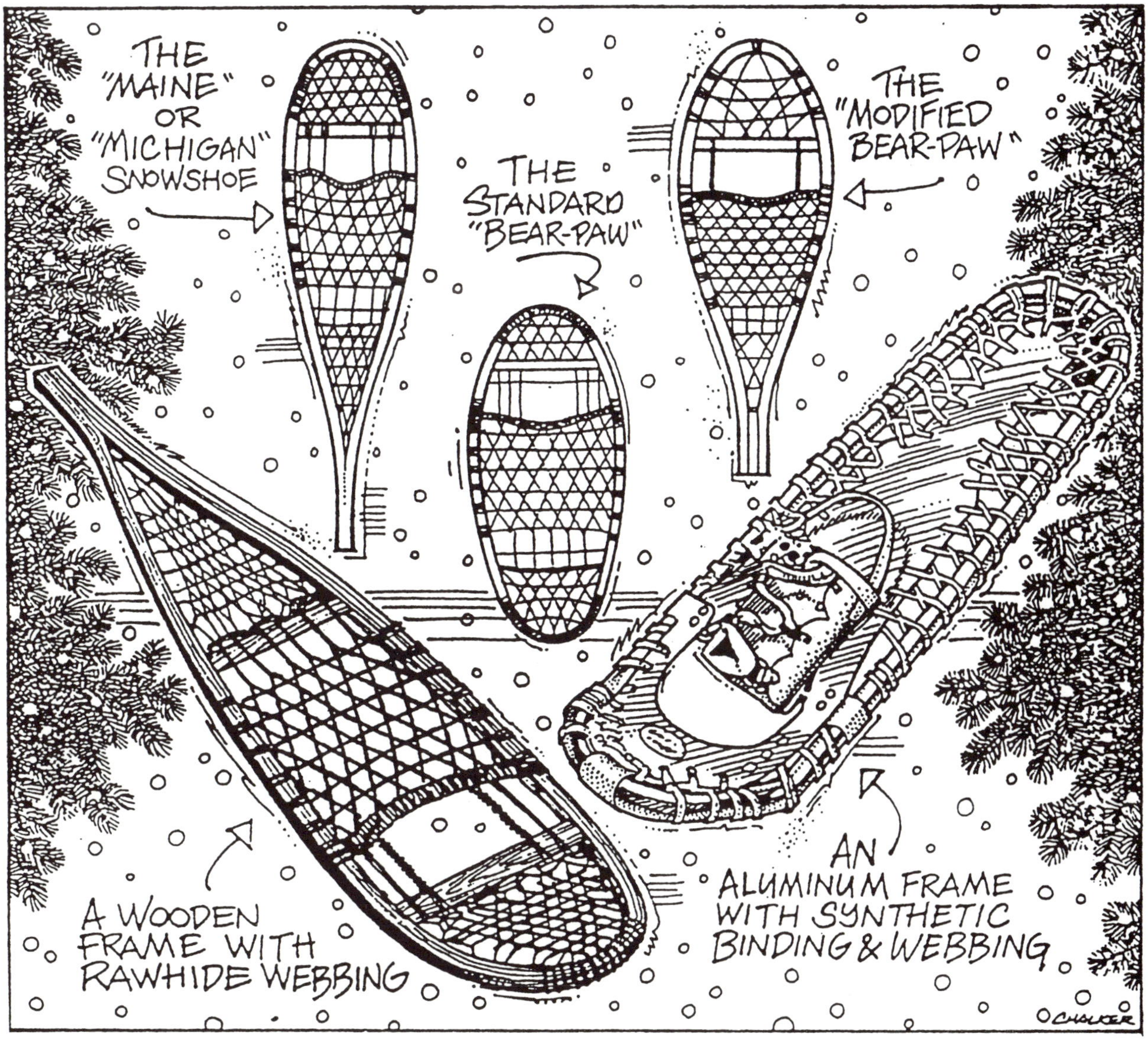

Knowing weather proverbs won't tell you where you are, but, like sticking a damp finger into the wind to find out the wind's direction, these old sayings may help you decipher Mother Nature's ways by reading her "signs" like an old Indian tracker. Never let it be said that you don't know enough to come in out of the rain or which way the wind is blowing.

'Red Sky at Night; Sailor's Delight'

By Hugh Westrup

Quick. What do fat skunks, cranky roosters, and Willard Scott have in common?

Give up? They all forecast the weather!

In the olden days, when there was no TV, and hence, no TV weather forecasters like Willard Scott, people looked elsewhere for weather forecasts. Often, they found their best clues in nature by observing plant or animal behavior or the color of the sky.

Frequently, these observations were put into the form of a saying or rhyme, which made them easier to remember. In time, hundreds of sayings about the weather were coined. Now, a physics professor from the University of Minnesota, Dr. George Freier, has put all the sayings together for the first time in a book called *Weather Proverbs*.

Dr. Freier's book is fascinating not only because he found so many weather proverbs, but also because he determined their accuracy in light of what modern meteorologists (weather scientists) know about the weather. Do fat skunks really foreshadow a long winter? Do roosters get cranky before a rain? Here is what Dr. Freier found out about the science behind different proverbs.

Aching Joints

When your joints all start to ache, rainy weather is at stake. It's a scientific fact that a drop or rise in barometric pressure usually accompanies a change in the weather. *Barometric pressure* refers to the force of the atmosphere as it pushes down on Earth's surface. In general, a cloudy sky occurs when the barometric pressure is low, and a clear sky occurs when the pressure is high.

"Open crocus, warm weather; closed crocus, cold weather." The crocus opens its petals in response to a rise in temperature. Botanists can actually tell the temperature by measuring how far a crocus has opened.

Dr. Freier says that a drop in air pressure has many effects on plants and animals. For example, when barometric pressure falls, the internal pressure of the human body adjusts to match the air pressure outside the body. If the internal pressure didn't change, it would become higher than the outside pressure, and the body would bulge.

When barometric pressure falls, dissolved gases in the blood are released as bubbles. These bubbles can irritate the nerves, causing itching, aches, and other forms of low-grade pain. Hence, the old saying about achy joints preceding rain.

If the rooster crows on going to bed, you may rise with a watery head. Other animals are also sensitive to barometric pressure, becoming irritable and noisy when the pressure falls. Birds, in particular, are noted for making a racket before a rain. This explains the rhyme about roosters crowing at bedtime.

Flowers smell best just before a rain. A change in the weather may also be preceded by a fluctuation in *humidity*, which is a measure of the amount of moisture in the air. As humidity increases, so does the probability of rain.

Humidity is also connected to the sense of smell. According to Dr. Freier, the human nose is stimulated by aromatic molecules given off by odorous things. Flowers smell because they emit aromatic molecules that float up upward and land inside the nose.

When it's humid outside, aromatic molecules are covered with a layer of water molecules. This watery layer makes the aromatic molecules cling more readily to the moist insides of the nose. Thus, an increase in humidity makes it easier to smell flowers, not to mention overpowering odors, such as swamp water and cow manure!

Insect Thermometers

Red sky at morning, sailor's warning; red sky at night, sailor's delight. Dr. Freier says this proverb is true only at times. It makes sense only when the morning sky is red in the west or the evening sky is red in the east.

Dr. Freier says a red sky indicates the presence of very humid air that contains huge drops of moisture that may fall later as rain. These drops are large enough to break up the rays of the sun, sending red light in the viewer's direction.

"Everything is lovely when the goose honks high." Geese fly at higher altitudes when the barometric pressure is high. Good weather usually occurs during times of high pressure.

Weather usually travels from west to east in the United States. Therefore, a red sky should serve as a warning only when it's in the west, indicating that humid air is coming your way. A red sky in the east is a delight because it means that the humid air has already passed by.

Count the number of cricket chirps in 14 seconds, add 40, and you have the temperature in degrees Fahrenheit. Suppose that you wanted to know what the temperature was outdoors, but you didn't have a thermometer. What would you do? Well, you might recall that many animals behave differently as the temperature changes. Cold-blooded animals—insects, reptiles, amphibians—are especially sensitive because their body temperature is determined by the temperature of the air around them.

Dr. Freier says that many weather proverbs focus on the activity of insects. Crickets, for example, make a chirping sound by sawing on their bodies with their back legs. The higher the temperature, the faster the insects saw. Hence, the above formula for finding the temperature by counting chirps.

"A ring around the sun or moon, means that rain will come real soon." A halo around the sun or moon appears when moonlight bounces off ice crystals high in the sky. These crystals are formed when moisture in warm, moist air freezes as the warmer air moves over colder air. The presence of moist, moving air suggests that rain or snow may soon be on the way.

Long Winter Ahead?

When skunks are real fat, we'll have a long winter coming. Most of the proverbs that Dr. Freier found are short-range predictions, which cover only a few days. There is a grain of truth in most short-range proverbs, he says.

Such is not the case, however, with long-range proverbs, which cover many months. Most weather systems last only a few days, so it is extremely difficult to predict weather months in advance. So when a fat skunk waddles by, the only thing you know for sure is that the skunk has been pigging out at mealtimes.

The study of proverbs is called *paroemiology*. Perhaps you have a weather proverb or two to add to Dr. Freier's list. If not, you could always make one up. In the coming months, make daily records of both the weather and other observations of natural phenomena. Then look back over your records for connections between simultaneous changes in weather and other events in nature. If successful, you might quality to be a paroemiologist.

Owls are master scanners of their environments who-o-o always know just where they are, and just what they are surveying. Of course, having a pair of binoculars and a compass helps these ardent orienteers to abbreviate vaster distances and shrink steeper depths.

Hiking Owls

Drawing by Lynn Munsinger

For a country to know which way is upward and onward it may have to glance backward upon its historical map that produced its icons, symbols and heritage. You can find out plenty about the United States by looking at the revered objects that have become "official" emblems of this heritage. All have stories behind them, and all transport and communicate pieces of the past into the future.

A Nation of Symbols

By Jan Boysen

Doug Sutherland is a man with a mission. He is determined to see the monarch butterfly declared America's official national insect. The orange-and-black beauty is a perfect choice, believes the Maryland entomologist. "Not only is it native to America, but the monarch is easily recognized, attractive and graceful," he says. "And its annual migration [a journey of 1,800 or more miles over several generations] makes it unique among insects."

A member of the Entomological Society of America, Sutherland actively campaigns for the butterfly, which lives and breeds in every state but Alaska. He has enlisted the support of environmental organizations and has lobbied Congress for legislation honoring the monarch. A born optimist, he hopes that in this centenary year of the Entomological Society, a butterfly bill will simply fly through the approval process.

If so, the monarch will join elite company. The only other living symbol of the United States is the rose, made the nation's official flower by act of Congress in 1986. The bald eagle, most people are surprised to learn, has never been granted official status as national bird, despite its selection, in 1782, for the national seal.

However, the monarch would flutter at the head of a long line of state insects, including the honeybee honored by Arkansas and six other states, and both the European and Carolina mantis, ladybug, California dog-faced butterfly, swallowtail butterfly and firefly favored by still other states. For while the national government has been slow to adopt official mascots, states have leapt at the chance to commemorate a host of animate and inanimate things, whether mammals or minerals, birds or bolo ties.

"Time was, each state had just two or three emblems from nature—an official flower and bird, and perhaps a tree," says Craig Tufts, director of urban wildlife programs for the National Wildlife Federation. No longer. While the growing list of commemoratives continues to include representatives from the natural world, man made objects with purely historical or economic significance are creeping onto the rosters of many states.

Maryland, for instance, has an official boat, the skipjack, a working sailboat used

by generations of Chesapeake Bay watermen. And just this year South Dakota's legislature approved a state musical instrument, the fiddle. But South Dakota's action is not original; Missouri lawmakers voted to embrace the fiddle two years ago.

Duplication of official items is common. Within the past two decades, eight states have selected milk as their official beverage. "Part of the replication can be tied to commercial interests, as with milk producers backing milk as the state beverage," explains Tufts. "In other cases it is the rapid flow of information today. One state gets an official beverage, and neighboring states hear about it."

In Massachusetts the beverage of choice is cranberry juice, no surprise given the economic importance of the state's cranberry bogs. Massachusetts also has the most emblems of any state—20 at last count. "We have an incredible number," admits Martha Clark, assistant to the state archivist, "but there is an easy answer. Massachusetts is one of the few states where individuals may petition the legislature, and their representative is duty-bound to bring up their bill." That translates into a plethora of petitions to commemorate the spirit of the Bay State.

In 1983, Massachusetts' spirit seemed to be hung up on rocks. Four different stony items were approved by the legislature: a state rock (Roxbury pudding-stone), state historic rock (Plymouth Rock), an explorer rock (Dighton rock) and a building stone (granite). And this in a state that already had proclaimed a state gem, a state mineral and a state fossil.

While some Massachusetts emblems are to be expected (the cod as state fish and the Boston bull terrier as state dog), Boston baked beans have not yet been commemorated. Nevertheless, there is a state muffin—the corn muffin. And Massachusetts is the only state with an official heroine, Deborah Samson, who fought in the Revolutionary War.

History has played a key role in the selection of several state symbols. Ohio's red carnation, the state flower, is firmly bound up with one of its favorite sons.

In his career as a politician, Ohio native William McKinley picked as his personal badge a newly developed variety of Old World pinks that we know as the carnation. As President of the United States, he often gave well-wishers carnation souvenirs. McKinley had handed a carnation to a small girl at the 1901 Pan American Exposition in Buffalo, New York, just moments before an assassin's bullet took his life. Two and a half years later, the Ohio legislature unanimously proclaimed the red carnation as state flower.

In Utah, a bird and a flower commemorate the heroic struggle faced by that state's early settlers. In 1848, Brigham Young's colony was on the verge of being devastated by an invasion of the dreaded "Mormon crickets." Many years later, historian Hubert Howe Bancroft portrayed the scene: "Vast swarms of crickets, black and baleful as the locusts of the Dead Sea left behind them not a blade or leaf. When everything was most disheartening, behold, from over the lake appeared myriads of snow-white gulls. They pounced upon the crickets, seizing and swallowing them . . . until the scourge was past."

No question but that the cricket-devouring California gull, despite its name, would become the state bird of Utah. Or that the sego lily would become the state flower; near starvation from the loss of crops to insects, the Mormon settlers learned from the Ute Indians how to dig, prepare and eat bulbs of the native lily.

Another bird prominent in history is Alabama's flicker. Locally called yellowhammer, its name was borrowed during the Civil War by a unit of nattily attired Alabama

Confederates who sported yellow epaulets on their uniforms. On one occasion, as those flashy troops marched in review before battle-weary, poorly attired compatriots in Kentucky, southern humorist Will Arnett catcalled: "Yellerhammer, yellerhammer, flicker, flicker!" The nickname stuck, and Alabamians acquired their state's avian symbol.

Delaware's blue hen mascot comes from the breed of chicken raised in Colonial days for cockfights; the Fighting Blue Hens were a unit of Kent County soldiers in the American Revolution. Rhode Island is the other state with a chicken for mascot—the colorful Rhode Island Red.

Game birds are the fowl of choice for several states. Pennsylvania's feathered mascot is the ruffed grouse, and South Dakota's is the ring-necked pheasant. Yet songbirds are the overwhelming favorites of most states. The cardinal is commemorated in seven states. Mockingbirds and meadowlarks each represent five others.

In general, flowers were the first natural symbols to be honored by state legislatures. The impetus was a resolution passed by a congress of women at the Chicago World's Columbian Exposition in 1893, calling for a "national garland" made up of flowers of the various states.

Soon state legislators were being visited by delegations from garden clubs and other groups lobbying for a particular flower. Within a few decades, the most popular blooms—violets and roses—had each been selected by four states. However, it has been the more distinctive blooms, such as the sunflower of Kansas and the bluebonnet of Texas, whose names have become most strongly identified with their respective states.

Not all commemoratives chosen from nature are living today. Lately a number of states have been adding official fossils. These run the gamut from huge dinosaurs like Colorado's stegosaurus to tiny sea creatures like the trilobites honored by Wisconsin, Pennsylvania and Ohio. Massachusetts

It started with flowers and birds, but now state rosters are getting crowded with all kinds of commemorative mascots.

commemorates a set of petrified dinosaur tracks.

And even living emblems may not exist today in the states they symbolize. California's grizzly, which first appeared on the flag of the California Republic in 1846, was extirpated in that state in 1922, three decades before it was even voted in as state animal. Hawaii's nene, the state bird, was once a candidate for extinction, although the wild goose hangs on thanks to an ambitious captive-breeding program.

Animals of all kinds continue to turn up on state rosters. The white-tailed deer is favored by five states, while three coastal ones have honored whales (the bowhead in Alaska, the sperm whale in Connecticut and the right whale in Georgia). State fish favorites include several species of trout and striped or largemouth bass, as well as Hawaii's humuhumunukunuk-a-pua'a, or triggerfish. Several states also grant recognition to reptiles, among them Florida and Louisiana, which have legally elevated the alligator to the status of official commemorative; there is also Arizona's ridgenosed rattlesnake, California's desert tortoise, Kansas' ornate box turtle and North Carolina's eastern box turtle. Only one state honors an amphibian, New Hampshire with its red-spotted newt.

With steady pushing from apiculturists, the European honeybee has won the favor of nine states for official insect. The bee's popularity has caused Doug Sutherland concern in his campaign for the monarch butterfly as national insect, although he is confident that once the honeybee's European origin is pointed out, Congress will rally round the all-American monarch.

And what about the more unusual commemoratives? Two states have official sports. Alaska honors dog mushing, in which dog teams and sledges recreate the historic winter transport of the Far North. Maryland's state sport is jousting, in which a rider on horseback attempts to drive a lance through a doughnut-shaped target—a nonviolent version of medieval knightly combat.

Three states have adopted an official dance, square dancing in both New Jersey and Washington, and the shag in South Carolina. Arizonans lack a dance but do have an official neckwear, the bolo tie.

Even after a state commemorative has been chosen, its fate always rests with legislatures, which retain the power to change them. In 1989, Montana lawmakers were asked to consider replacing their migratory state bird, the western meadowlark, with a species, the black-billed magpie, that sticks around the entire year. Despite the apparent logic in parting company with an inconstant bird that prefers to winter in warmer climes, "The bill was rejected heartily," reports Ellie Arguimbau, a librarian for the Montana Historical Society. "Anyone who has listened to the lyrical song of the meadowlark and compared it with the magpie's raucous call should well know why!"

4

INTO THE WOODS

Myths have always helped people understand the world around them when they didn't have what we call that old-time religion or what we consider hard, cold facts. This article and the two that follow explore some commonly held beliefs about forests and their inhabitants. "I think that I shall never see a poem as lovely as a tree" wrote Joyce Kilmer, but answer this: Where else would you hang a swing? Or build a tree house, count stars in a night sky, and whistle like a bird?

Sacred Trees and Magical Forests

By Robert D. San Souci

In many societies, trees have long been regarded as objects of wonder, magic, and power. For some peoples, the tree represented the fertile power of the earth with its endless cycle of rebirth and renewal. The seed that was buried in the earth brought forth new life, and the tree that lost its leaves in the fall and appeared dead during the cold winter suddenly came alive again in spring.

The ancient Mesopotamians in western Asia saw their kings as caretakers of the Tree of Life because the king was regarded as the people's link to the divine powers of fertility and growth. In Egypt, where great forests were unknown, the sycamore tree represented the Great Earth Mother, who nurtured all living things. Today traces of the age-old worship of trees linger in customs such as the Christmas tree, which reminds people in winter of the promise of spring. The maypole harks back to decorating a tree in the village square to bring the fertility of nature to the town.

The Romans honored the great mother goddess, Cybele, with a pine tree brought in yearly to her temple. The Romans also believed that Jupiter was sheltered under an oak tree when he was an infant. Further north, in Scandinavia, the oak was sacred to the Norse god Thor.

Trees have played key roles, with both positive and negative aspects, in religious traditions around the world. Buddha found enlightenment under the Bodhi tree, but Adam and Eve were cast out of paradise because they ate the fruit of a certain tree forbidden to them by the Lord. Among the Sioux Indians of North America, a sacred cottonwood tree was the focus of the sun dance, which put them in touch with the sacred world.

The Norsemen viewed the whole universe in terms of the great world tree Yggdrasil, whose roots extended to the underworld, whose trunk grew through the world of mortals, and whose branches reached into heaven. The ancient Aztecs, in what is now Mexico, talked of a cosmic tree that sprang from the body of the earth goddess, linking the earthly and heavenly realms.

Trees still play a symbolic role in many customs concerning birth, marriage, and death. In parts of the Soviet Union, Germany, France, England, Italy, and Switzerland, it is customary to plant and bless a tree when the child of an important citizen is baptized. Some Swiss people still plant an apple tree for a boy and a pear tree for a girl.

Until the last century, in Germany and some eastern European countries, a "marriage tree" would be planted near the house of a newly married couple. In rural India, newlyweds still walk around a special tree several times in the hope of taking into themselves the fertile power of the tree.

Some American Indian tribes suspended their dead in boxes tied to the branches of trees with cedar-bark ropes, perhaps with the idea that the tree would give new life to the dead body. Even today, it is common to plant a tree in memory of someone who has died.

For many peoples, trees had spirits and could often take on human shapes. Stories from Europe and Asia tell of trees (often willows) that became beautiful women. In New Zealand, among the Maori, the *ti* palms of the Kaingaroa Plains were believed to be women transformed into trees. It was said these trees could move about, making them unreliable guideposts for a traveler.

A related idea, also widespread, was the belief that trees sheltered the souls of the dead. The Egyptians believed that the souls of the recently deceased took the forms of birds in the sacred sycamore. In Korea, only the souls of those who died violently entered the trees, while in France it was held that trees harbored the souls of those condemned to repay some sin.

When thousands of trees cluster together to make a forest, their power can become far more awesome. Forests are places of mystery and shadow, where the rules of the everyday world no longer hold and wild plants grow so thickly that they can blot out the light of the sun. In contrast to cities or plains and meadows, the deep, dark forest was a place of magic and danger, inhabited by gods, evil spirits, and a host of other curious creatures such as nymphs and satyrs.

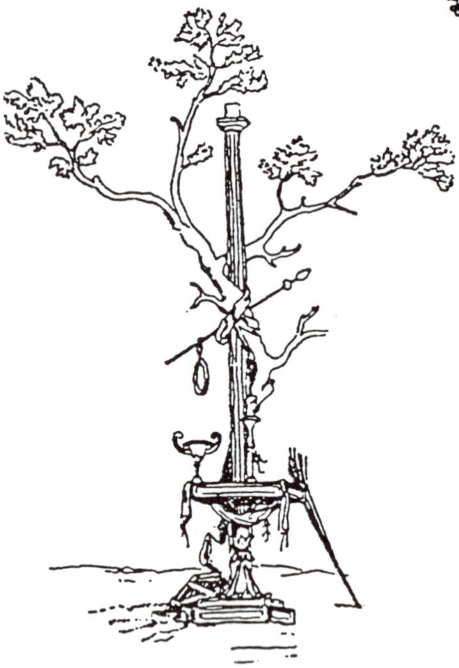

Roman sacred tree and sacrificial table

Wood nymph

In Papua New Guinea, some people feared the Kilyakai—tiny forest demons believed to shoot poisoned arrows that caused malaria in travelers. In the Baltic countries of northern Europe, the Leshy were thought to move tree trunks around and fill in a wanderer's tracks in the snow so that unfortunate people would plunge ever deeper into the wintry woods. In England, legends tell of the Green Man, often described as having tree trunks for legs and leafy branches for arms, who would pounce on unsuspecting travelers.

Countless fairy tales by the Brothers Grimm and others tell how heroes or heroines have had to go into the woods to meet a princess or prince, to overcome a witch or ogre, or to find a treasure or the entrance to fairyland. The Teton Sioux tell of a hunter who meets and fights a skeleton in a haunted forest. In Russian folktales, the woods are where one meets wizards and vampires, monsters and the magical firebird. Because the forest inspired such mystery, awe, and even terror, woodland groves were among the first places in nature dedicated to the gods.

Holy stands of trees were familiar among the Greeks, Romans, Celts, and Persians, as well as throughout Asia, Africa, and America. Among the ancient Germanic peoples, anyone who even dared to peel the bark off a tree in a sacred grove was severely punished. Some peoples maintained holy groves near their villages or dwellings. Those who believed that trees and groves had spirits dwelling in them would have to perform special ceremonies when they cut down a tree in order to appease the spirit or encourage it to go elsewhere.

Today woodlands are very much in the news as concerned people work to save the rain forests and the remaining old-growth forests of the world. While many people no longer view trees and woods as the dwelling places of spirits and strange beings, we are reminded just how important the forests are to the earth. They play an important role in producing the very air we breathe. Just as importantly, they remain places of natural beauty where we can get in touch with the renewing powers of the earth and open timeless doors on worlds of the imagination.

Next time you have an urge to call your younger brother "birdbrain," get wise to what other people have thought about birds, and be glad that you know better. Carol Gelber tells you about real and imaginary birds, like the phoenix that dies then rises again, a story with a perpetual happy ending.

Beliefs About Birds

By Carol Gelber

Birds have long fascinated humans with their gorgeous feathers and lovely songs. In cooler parts of the world, many birds appear suddenly in the spring and vanish in the fall. Indeed, their ability to fly has made birds the objects of awe and envy.

Because birds can soar out of sight into "heaven" or "never-never land," they have often been connected with supernatural sky powers. In myth and folklore, birds are messengers of heavenly gods (or sometimes the gods themselves, in disguise) or bearers of secret information. Even today, when we do not want to reveal where we heard a secret, we say, "A little bird told me!"

Phoenix

We have not always known that many birds migrate long distances between their summer and winter homes. In the past, people wondered where the birds went in the winter. One belief, first proposed in ancient Greece, was that birds, like bears, hibernated. Swallows were thought to bury themselves in the mud of riverbanks and sleep through the cold winter. Until recent times, many Europeans believed that large birds such as cranes and storks carried tiny songbirds on their backs to winter in tropical Africa.

One solution to the mystery of migration was proposed in a paper published in 18th-century London. The author declared that if birds flew away parallel to the ground, travelers would be able to spot flocks of them overhead. Ignoring evidence to the contrary, he claimed that great flocks of birds were never seen traveling together. Thus, he argued, the birds must fly perpendicular to the earth. And where do they land? On the moon, of course. He calculated that the trip to and from the moon took four months, leaving the birds plenty of time for a winter lunar holiday.

Because of their migratory habits, birds remind us that spring has arrived or that summer is over. Americans say that spring is coming when they see the first robin. In England, the cuckoo is the symbol of spring, and in many parts of Europe and Asia, its loudly repeated call was believed to forecast rain.

In superstition and myth, birds predict not only the seasons and weather but also the future. In Germany, girls would ask the cuckoo to tell them how many years would pass before they would marry. The Danes said it was no wonder the cuckoo (which lays its eggs in other birds' nests) did not build its own nest—it was too busy answering people's questions.

Some birds, like owls, have been considered omens of disaster. Perhaps the owl's bad reputation comes from its habit of hunting at night, when it may screech or hoot mournfully from the dark woods.

Other birds, such as the fierce, keen-sighted eagle, are associated with good fortune, bravery, and personal importance. The ancient Romans regarded the eagle as the personification of Jupiter, the king of the gods. A silver eagle with outspread wings and thunderbolts in its claws was carried at the head of Roman armies. In fact, countries have chosen the eagle as their symbol more often than any other bird. The U.S. Congress adopted the bald eagle as our national emblem [seal] in 1782.

North American Indians also held the eagle in high regard. The Zuni of the Southwest believed that eagles entered a hole in the sky when they soared out of sight. They kept captured eagles in rooftop cages in order to use the feathers. Among the Indians, eagle feathers were a symbol of importance usually worn only by chiefs and war leaders.

In myth and legend, birds are often protectors of people. The quetzal, a rare bird of the mountains of Central America, is the national bird of Guatemala, whose second largest city is called Quetzaltenango, or "Place of the Quetzal." The male quetzal is a lovely glittering green except for its breast and belly, which are bright crimson. A long tail, iridescent with blue or violet, ripples behind it when it flies. The Maya of ancient Mexico considered the quetzal a sacred bird that protected their chiefs, and the punishment for killing one was death.

In designs of the woodland Indians of the Great Lakes region, the mythical thunderbird takes the shape of an eaglelike bird. The jagged lines above the birds represent lightning.

According to Mayan legend, the quetzal was once an all-green bird. An emerald-colored quetzal hovered over the head of a chieftain who battled the Spanish conquistador Pedro de Alvarado. The bird flew at the Spanish invader, pecking at him with its beak. Unfortunately, Alvarado had a horse and armor, and the quetzal was powerless to stop him from spearing and killing the Mayan chief with his iron lance. The bird spread its shimmering wings over the dead chief's body, and by the next morning, when the quetzal flew off into the forest, its breast had been stained blood red, the color it remains today.

While fanciful beliefs surround real birds such as eagles, cuckoos, and quetzals, some birds are completely imaginary. Perhaps the best known is the phoenix. First described by a Greek historian in the fifth century B.C., it was said to live more than 500 years. Only one phoenix existed at any time. When it was ready to die, it built a nest of fragrant spices and then burst into flames. When the fire cooled, a brand-new phoenix rose from the ashes. Today we use the phoenix as a symbol of hope for a new beginning after a disaster. In fact, one insurance company uses a phoenix as its company emblem.

Belief in a thunderbird that was responsible for rainstorms was common among North American Indians. The Haida Indians of Alaska said that when a storm approached and the sky grew dark, it was because the thunderbird had stretched its wings over the sun. Every time the bird flapped its wings, thunder rumbled and lightning flashed from its eyes. On its back, this giant bird carried a lake that it would pour out in a torrent of rain.

Even people who no longer believe in birds with magical powers or in the existence of imaginary birds say that they are looking for "the bluebird of happiness." And we may call someone "proud as a peacock," "a wise old owl," or "a silly goose." Bird symbols still represent our deepest feelings of joy, fear, and pride.

The first time this story was told was probably in the forests of old Russia. It's a familiar story—three brothers, a quest, an elusive treasure—but in this one, the hero dies. Not to worry, there is still room for a wedding and maybe even another happy ending.

The Firebird

Retold by Sam Dustin

Illustrated by Robin Hansen-Cole

Long ago in a faraway tzardom lived Tzar Vislaff Andronovich. He had three sons—Dimitri, Vassilii, and Ivan. The tzar also had a magnificent garden in which a tree that bore golden apples grew.

One day the tzar noticed that his golden apples were disappearing. Soon he learned that the Firebird, a bird with feathers of gold and eyes like crystals, was coming to the garden at night and stealing the apples. Outraged, the tzar summoned his three sons and promised his tzardom to whichever one could capture the Firebird.

The first night, Dimitri kept watch in the garden, but he fell asleep and did not see the Firebird come and steal the apples. The second night, Vassilii watched for the bird. He, too, fell asleep, and in the morning, more apples were gone.

The third night, it was Ivan's turn. He waited several hours for the bird. Suddenly, the garden was filled with light, and Ivan could see the Firebird perched in the apple tree. Without a sound, he climbed to within reach of the bird and grasped its tail feathers. But he could not hold on to the Firebird, which flew away, leaving Ivan holding a single golden feather.

In the morning, Ivan showed his father the feather and told him about the Firebird. The tzar was determined to have the bird, but after its encounter with Ivan, it stopped coming to the garden.

Again the tzar summoned his sons. This time he asked them to go in search of the Firebird. "The one who brings it to me will have what I have already promised," he said.

Dimitri and Vassilii, jealous of Ivan and the praise he received for getting one of the Firebird's feathers, left without their younger brother, and Ivan had to set out alone. After riding for many hours, he reached a clearing. There he found a post inscribed with information about the three roads that branched off ahead: "He who rides straight on will be cold and hungry. He who rides to the left will be well, but his horse will die. He who rides to the right will be killed, but his horse will live."

Ivan considered his choices and took the road to the left. He rode for three days. On the third day, a Gray Wolf appeared and said, "You read the post, so you know that your horse must die." No sooner had the wolf said this than he devoured Ivan's horse.

Now Ivan had to continue his journey on

foot. Toward the end of the day, he met up with the Gray Wolf again. "I feel sorry for you," the wolf said. "Climb on my back, and I will take you wherever you must go."

Ivan told the wolf of his errand, and swift as the wind, they were off. The wolf stopped at a high stone wall and told Ivan that he would find the Firebird on the other side. "Take only the bird and leave the cage, or you will be caught," the wolf said.

The bird was there in a beautiful golden cage. Forgetting the wolf's words, Ivan reached for the cage. As soon as he touched it, a great alarm rang out, and watchmen appeared and seized the startled boy.

Ivan was taken to the ruler of that land, Tzar Dolmat, who was furious to learn of the attempted theft. Ivan explained who he was and why he wanted the Firebird. Tzar Dolmat answered, "If you had asked me for the Firebird, I would have given it to you. Now I must proclaim you a thief. But I will spare you if you will go to the tzardom of Tzar Affron and bring me his Golden-Maned Horse. If you do this, I will give you the Firebird and the cage, and I will say nothing of your theft."

Ivan went to the Gray Wolf and explained what had happened. "You should have listened to my advice," the wolf said. "But I will help you again. Climb on my back, and I will take you wherever you must go."

The wolf ran until they reached the stables of Tzar Affron. "Take the Golden-Maned Horse but leave the bridle that hangs next to it, for it will bring you harm," the wolf advised.

Ivan took the horse, but when he saw the beautiful golden bridle, he could not resist taking that, too. The moment Ivan touched it, a noise like thunder sounded, and instantly he was seized by guards.

Tzar Affron listened to Ivan's story and agreed to spare him if he would go to the tzardom where the tzarevna Helena the Beautiful lived and bring her to him. If he did this, Ivan could have the Golden-Maned Horse.

Once again, Ivan asked the Gray Wolf for help, and again the wolf took him to where he had to go. When they reached the garden of Tzarevna Helena, the wolf told Ivan to wait for him down the road. The wolf hid in the bushes, and when the tzarevna took her evening walk, he caught her by surprise. With the tzarevna on his back, the wolf ran to where Ivan was waiting.

As they neared the tzardom of Tzar Affron, Ivan said sadly, "Oh, Wolf, I have fallen in love with the beautiful tzarevna, and now I have to exchange her for a horse! If I don't, I will be declared a thief and will not be given the Firebird."

"I can help you, Ivan," said the wolf. Suddenly, the wolf transformed himself into a perfect likeness of Tzarevna Helena.

"Take me to Tzar Affron in place of the real tzarevna," he said. "Then escape with Helena on the Golden-Maned Horse. When you have gone a safe distance, think of me, and I will be by your side."

Ivan did as he was told. After a while, he thought of his friend, and the Gray Wolf appeared immediately. They continued on toward the tzardom of Tzar Dolmat.

When they drew near Tzar Dolmat's palace, Ivan realized that he had grown so attached to the Golden-Maned Horse that he could not bear to give it away. Sensing Ivan's unhappiness, the Gray Wolf said, "Ivan, I know you want to keep the Golden-Maned Horse, and I can help you." As he said this, he transformed himself into a golden-maned horse that was identical to the real one. Ivan presented the false horse to Tzar Dolmat and in return received the Firebird in its golden cage.

Ivan left the palace with the Firebird and went to where he had left Helena the Beautiful and the Golden-Maned Horse. Ivan thought of the Gray Wolf, and they were at once reunited. They traveled together until they reached the place where Ivan had first met the wolf.

"Ivan, I have served you well," the wolf said. "Now I bid you farewell." With that, the Gray Wolf ran off.

Ivan rode on toward home with Helena by his side. Exhausted by the journey, they stopped to rest and soon fell asleep. As they slept, Dimitri and Vassilii happened upon the couple. Seeing the beautiful tzarevna, the Golden-Maned Horse, and the Firebird, the brothers decided to kill Ivan and steal his treasures.

Dimitri drew his sword and stabbed Ivan to death. Vassilii awakened Helena and said, "We shall take you to our father, and you must tell him that we won you, the Golden-Maned Horse, and the Firebird. If you do not do as I say, we shall kill you!" Too frightened to disobey their orders, Tzarevna Helena went with them.

For 30 days, Ivan lay where he had been slain. On the 31st day, the Gray Wolf happened to pass by and found him. He was anxious to help his friend, but he needed assistance. Spotting a raven flying overhead, he called, "Raven, listen to me and do as I say. Fly to the ends of the earth and fetch me some of the waters of Life and Death."

The raven flew away and in three days returned with two acorns filled with the waters. The Gray Wolf sprinkled Ivan's body with the water of Death, and his wounds healed. He sprinkled Ivan's face with the water of Life, and Ivan jumped to his feet, rubbed his eyes, and said, "Have I been asleep?"

"Yes, my friend," the wolf said. "And you would have slept forever if I had not come by. But now we must hurry to your father's house, for Helena the Beautiful is going to marry your brother Vassilii, and you must prevent it."

The wolf sped off with Ivan on his back. They arrived at the palace just as the wedding was about to begin. When Helena saw Ivan, she ran to him crying, "Here is my brave knight."

When Tzar Vislaff Andronovich heard Ivan's story, he ordered his guards to throw Dimitri and Vassilii into the dungeon. Ivan and Helena the Beautiful were married that same day, and they spent the rest of their lives together in happiness.

This and the following two entries about leeches and mistletoe are about healing. You may be surprised to learn that before there was aspirin, there were trees to provide relief from common ailments such as toothaches or to appease a sweet tooth. But before you start gnawing on a tree, make sure you can identify it correctly. Chewing on the wrong one could be enough to make your sap run.

Helpful Trees

By E. Barrie Kavasch

Centuries ago, the Iroquois Indians (Haudenosaunee) called the people who lived in the nearby mountains Adirondacks ("Bark Eaters") because they ate inner tree bark. Our forests have fed, healed, sheltered, and warmed people since they first arrived in this hemisphere, and different kinds of trees and shrubs give special kinds of help, such as the following:

Tree/Shrub	***Provides***	***Used For***
Maple	Wood splints and sap	Baskets, syrup, and sugar
Ash	Wood splints and wood	Baskets and baseball bats
Oak	Wood splints, acorns, and bark	Baskets, food, and yellow dye
Hickory	Outer bark, nuts, and wood splints	Baskets, food, flavoring and smoke curing
Prickly ash	Twigs and bark	Relief of toothache
Willow	Inner bark	Aspirin-like pain relief
Mesquite	Pods, beans, and bark	Food, fiber, and smoke curing
Witch hazel	Bark and twigs	Astringent and poison-ivy treatment
Kentucky coffee	Seeds	Coffee substitute
Joshua	Roots and leaves	Fiber and soap
Persimmon	Fruit	Foods and preservatives
Piñon	Seeds and resin	Foods and gum

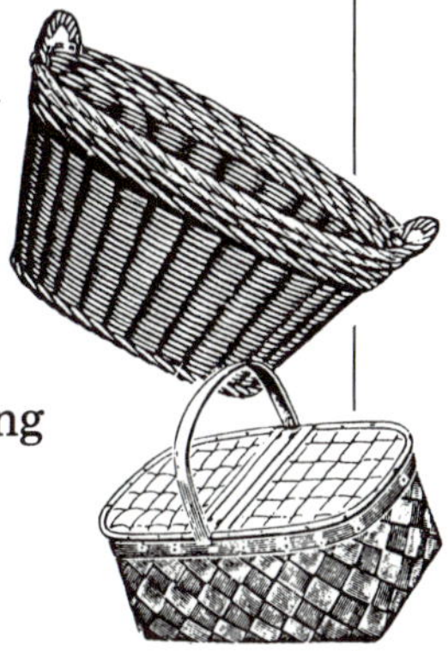

You're about to discover that before mistletoe hangs from your ceiling during Christmas time, it lives on a tree, gloriously sapping its strength. There's more to mistletoe than smooching, but, if you get bit by a snake over the holidays, don't reach for a sprig—it's not true that it is a cure.

All About Mistletoe

By Carol Viens

No one knows when the custom of kissing under the mistletoe began. Most of us, however, are familiar with the bunches of dark green leaves and pearly white berries that decorate doorways every Christmas. There are many myths and legends about mistletoe. In medieval times sprigs of it were worn as good luck charms against evil spirits. Often it was hung over doorways all year long to make sure that only good luck entered the house. African warriors of the Walos tribe carried mistletoe when they went into battle. They believed it would keep them safe from harm.

For hundreds of years the leaves and berries of the mistletoe were thought to have special healing powers. Juice from the berries was used in Japan, Switzerland, and Cambodia. American Indians of the Southwest thought it cured ailments ranging from coughs to snakebite. In more modern times mistletoe has been used for the treatment of nerve disorders and in cancer research.

Large clumps of mistletoe can sometimes be seen clinging to the branches of oak or pine trees. It may look pretty, but the

mistletoe is actually killing the tree on which it lives. It is a parasite. That is, it lives off other plants, called host plants. Mistletoe steals food, moisture, vitamins, and minerals from the host plants, making them dry out and lose their strength. If allowed to grow, it can severely damage or even kill a tree in a few short years.

The leaves and branches of the mistletoe have been used to feed cattle and sheep. Many wild animals, such as deer and elk, get nourishment from its leaves during the harsh winter months when food is difficult to find.

Although birds can eat mistletoe berries with safety, these same berries are poisonous to people. Never try to taste a mistletoe berry. If you see a younger child put one into his mouth, stop him and remove it. Just one of those pretty white berries is enough to make you extremely ill.

Mistletoe has an interesting history and can be enjoyed for its beauty, but save your appetite for holiday turkey.

If you've read "Helpful Trees," you may be getting used to the idea of odd cures. Leeches, say, from lakes or forest streams, have their uses that are worth including here. After centuries of being ostracized by the medical community, leeches are "in" again.

Take Two Leeches and Call Me in the Morning

By D. M. Souza

Bloodsucking leeches came to the rescue of a Massachusetts boy not long ago.

A dog had bitten the boy's ear off. Days after a Boston surgeon reattached the ear, blood stopped flowing through it and the tissue was in danger of dying. That's when the surgeon, Dr. Joseph Upton, turned to leeches for help.

He placed two leeches on the problem area. They pierced the skin and went to work. Gradually the blood started to circulate properly. In a few days, the boy left the hospital with his ear intact.

Leeches are becoming useful tools for microsurgery, a procedure that connects tiny blood vessels to one another. The leeches can help when the vessels get clogged with clotted blood.

When a leech attaches its suction-disk mouth to the area, three blade-like teeth painlessly pierce the skin. To make the blood easier to suck, the leech then injects an "anticoagulant" chemical that keeps the blood from thickening. This anti-clotting chemical is what Dr. Upton needed. It breaks up blocked areas, allowing veins to branch out and blood to flow. The leech, in return for its help, gets about a teaspoon of blood to eat.

Use of leeches is catching on in the United States. Recently, several plastic surgeons have used the creatures while reattaching fingers, toes, and flaps of skin. Doctors have also found them helpful to treat bruises.

"There's nothing like a leech for a badly swollen black eye," says Dr. Charles Lent, a scientist who's been studying medicinal leeches for 15 years.

Using leeches in medicine is not new. More than a century ago, leeches were used to treat everything from indigestion to pneumonia. Physicians wrongly believed that the bloodsuckers could draw out whatever was causing the sickness.

Leeches are found the world over in

streams, lakes and ponds, even in salt water. They can swim upside down, crawl like inchworms across rocks, and tread water. Commonly, they are olive green and brown, and measure only two to five centimeters long. The medicinal type can reach 20 centimeters in length. A hundred years ago, people harvested leeches by wading in ponds and allowing them to attach to their legs. Today, medicinal leeches are grown in laboratory farms.

In addition to surgeons, scientists are finding leeches useful. Researchers study their nervous systems, which are similar to human nerves. Other scientists are trying to find ways to use leech secretions to treat heart disease.

The leech may have a promising future in science and medicine. Leeches USA Ltd., of Long Island, N.Y., reports it sold 20,000 to hospitals and labs last year; and demand for the little suckers keeps growing.

TIMBER! What happens to trees when they are cut down? Good things, in this article and the one called "A Bat Is Born." Here, David's father makes a totem pole, carving away anything that is not part of the pictures he "sees" in its wood. You can learn more about David and his father in the book, Totem Pole, *by Diane Hoyt-Goldsmith.*

Totem Pole Boy

By Deborah H. DeFord

Illustrated by Mike DiGiorgio

David Boxley and his father walk through the woods. They are looking for the perfect tree. It must be a cedar tree. It must be tall and straight. It should not have many branches.

David and his father are Indians. David's father is also an artist. He carves wood. He and David are looking for a tree to carve into a totem pole. When the totem pole is finished, it will tell the story of their Indian tribe.

David's father cuts down the tree they find. He cuts off all the branches. Then David's father tells David that he sees pictures hidden in the wood of the tree. He carves the wood until the pictures appear.

What pictures does David's father see? He sees pictures from the tribe's history. The pictures may be people of the tribe. Or they may be animals.

David is proud to be a member of his tribe. And he's proud to be the son of the woodcarver who tells the story of his tribe on a tall cedar tree.

Your Very Own TOTEM POLE

Here's how to make a tabletop totem pole that tells a story about you.

What you need:

- 5 empty spools used for thread
- pencil for drawing
- white construction paper
- colored markers
- scissors
- white glue
- 3-inch square of cardboard
- unsharpened pencil
- cellophane tape

What you do:

1. Using a pencil, draw a picture on each spool. Each picture should tell something about you. Here are some ideas for things to draw:
   - your favorite animal
   - a character from your favorite story
   - your best friend
   - your favorite teacher
   - the oldest person in your family

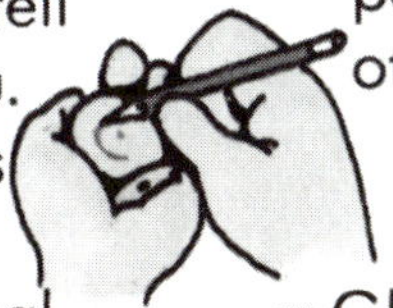

2. On construction paper, draw a pencil picture of a bird that visits your neighborhood.

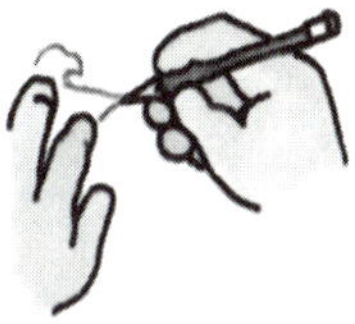

3. Use colored markers to make all your pencil drawings bright. Cut out your paper bird.

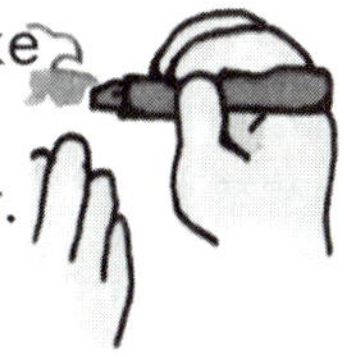

4. Glue the bottom of one spool to the cardboard square.

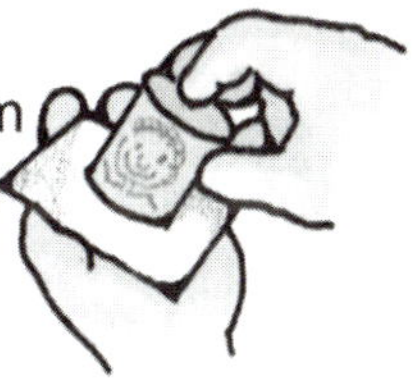

5. Place the unsharpened pencil in the hole of the spool.

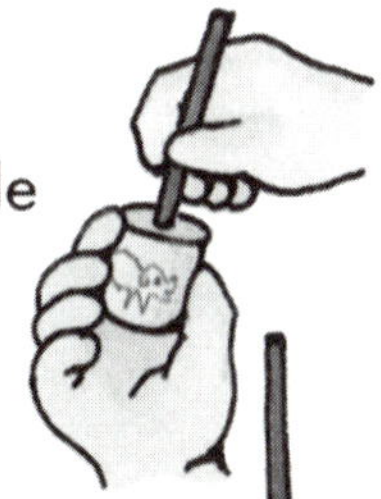

6. Glue the remaining spools in a stack atop the first spool.

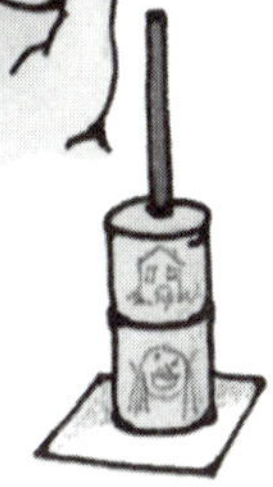

7. Tape the bird picture to the top of the pencil.

Illustration by Mike DiGiorgio

TIMBER, TOO! (See "Totem Pole Boy.") Baseball bats are inside ash trees, just waiting to be carved free of all that additional wood (à la a man called Michelangelo, and we don't mean a Ninja turtle!) and let loose on the ball field. The care that goes into their creation would make even a Renaissance sculptor happy. Among ball players, a new bat may mean another chance to make a winning hit.

A Bat Is Born

By Marc Appleman

Eric Davis, the slugging centerfielder of the Cincinnati Reds, is waiting for a special delivery. It's 34 inches long and weighs 31 ounces. It's strong, smooth and solid, and it smells like it just came out of a lumberyard. It's a C271 model Louisville Slugger baseball bat.

"My bat is like a brother to me. That's how close I feel to it," says Eric. "And you have to take care of it. You cater to its every need. You clean it. You don't throw it. You keep a close eye on a good bat. And you're always kind of sad when you break it."

Broken bats have to be replaced, and by the time a new bat reaches Eric at Riverfront Stadium, the Reds home ballpark, it will have completed a long journey. It takes a lot longer for a piece of northern white ash wood to make it to the big leagues than it took Eric to arrive there.

Eric was born in 1962. The tree that was used to make his bat was already growing in 1927, the year Babe Ruth hit 60 home runs for the New York Yankees. It grew in a forest in northern Pennsylvania, where the soil and annual rainfall are just right for growing the northern white ash trees that are used to make the best wood bats. Ash has the right combination of strength, flexibility and weight to send a well-hit baseball more than 400 feet.

Good Wood

A tree has to be at least 60 years old before its wood is mature enough to be used to make a bat. After a tree has been cut down and had its branches stripped, it is shipped to a nearby mill and inspected. Only the very best wood is used to make bats for major league players, so sometimes just two or three major league bats are made from one tree. Wood that has knots or an uneven grain is used for bats sold at sporting goods stores and for making furniture. New trees are always sprouting to replace the trees that have been cut down.

Once the wood for Eric's bat is approved at the mill, it is cut into 40-inch-long pieces called billets, which look like round fence posts. The billets are sent by truck from Pennsylvania to "Slugger Park" in Jeffersonville, Indiana, where the Hillerich &

Bradsby Company makes Louisville Slugger bats.

There are many kinds of bats made around the world, but the Louisville Slugger is the most popular brand, and it has been around the longest. The first Louisville Slugger was made in 1884! Last year, 1,500,000 Louisville Sluggers were made, and almost 200,000 of them were for major league baseball players.

Slugger Park

Freshly cut wood is very moist, so the billets must be dried out in a type of oven called a kiln before they can be turned into bats.

The dried billets are inspected and weighed and sent to the production room at Slugger Park. Sawdust covers the floor, and many stacks of bats and billets fill the huge room, which has an 11-foot-long bat hanging from the ceiling for decoration. This factory seems like a combination of a lumberyard, toy store and ballpark!

Only wood bats are made here. Aluminum bats are now very popular in recreational leagues, schools and colleges because they almost never break. But major and minor league baseball players are still required to use wood bats. When Eric became a pro, he had to switch from aluminum to wood.

"Aluminum bats are lighter, and they are easier to hit with," says Eric. "Switching from aluminum bats to wood was the

MARK ALEXANDER PHOTOGRAPHY, CINCINNATI, OH.

Eric Davis sits with baseball bats from his own private collection of Louisville Sluggers.

In the Slugger Park timber yard, billets of northern white ash wait to be placed in kilns for the drying out or seasoning process.

COURTESY HILLERICH & BRADSBY CO., LOUISVILLE, KY.

The new owner of this baseball bat requires one that is shorter than the metal template from which it was modeled. Here, a worker in the Slugger Park factory "cuts off" the bat by hand until it is the exact length required by the new owner. This kind of special attention has been given to Louisville Sluggers for over 100 years.

COURTESY HILLERICH & BRADSBY CO., LOUISVILLE, KY.

toughest adjustment I ever had to make." He sure has made the adjustment successfully! In his first four full major league seasons, Eric batted .281, hit 124 home runs and drove in 365 runs.

A lot of people get involved when Eric needs new bats. The Reds equipment manager sends an order to Hillerich & Bradsby, and factory workers read the order on a computer terminal in the production room.

Eric wants bats that are 34 inches long and weigh 31 ounces. Many major leaguers use bats of that size. Some players, though, use very different sized bats. Bobby Bonilla, the Pittsburgh Pirates rightfielder, uses a 35-inch 35-ounce bat. Marty Barrett, the Boston Red Sox second baseman, uses a bat that weighs only 28 ounces!

Getting in Shape

To make Eric's bat, a worker uses a machine called a tracer lathe. On one part of the tracer lathe, he mounts a wood billet that has the proper weight and grain quality to become Eric's bat. On another part of the lathe, he places a metal template, or pattern, that has the exact shape that Eric's bat will have. As the billet spins rapidly, a very sharp blade follows the curves of the template, cutting wood from the billet until Eric's bat has taken shape. It takes only 10 seconds to shape each bat!

Eric's bat is weighed when it comes off the tracer lathe. "An ounce can make a big difference," Eric says. Eric uses his C271 model during spring training and during the first part of the season, when he feels really strong. But later in the summer, when it gets hot and he has already played in a lot of games, Eric often switches to an I13C model. With a smaller head and thinner handle, the I13C is about an ounce lighter. Sometimes, Eric will switch to a lighter bat in the seventh inning of a game because he is tired from running the bases and chasing down balls in centerfield.

Once Eric's bat has taken shape, it goes to a branding machine. A smell of burning wood fills the air as Eric's bat passes over a red-hot brand. The bat is branded with the Louisville Slugger trademark; the C271 model number; the number 125, which means that the best timber was used to make the bat; and, of course, Eric's signature. The trademark is always branded on the weakest part of the bat. By keeping the part with the trademark away from the ball, batters can be sure that they are hitting with the strongest wood.

Eric's bat next goes to another worker and another machine, where the scorch marks from the branding fire are removed.

The people who work in the factory get very excited knowing that the bat they are working on today might soon be hitting home runs for Eric. They hope Eric will treat it with the same care that they put into making it. Last season, when Bo Jackson of the Kansas City Royals broke a bat over his knee because he was frustrated, some bat makers got mad. "He broke the bat because he struck out," said Ronald Bryant, the production supervisor. "It's not the bat's fault when he strikes out!"

The next stop for Eric's bat is the combination machine, where it is sanded smooth and the end nubs that held the bat in place during the lathing are removed. At this point, a lot of major league bats are dipped in clear lacquer or black paint and hung to dry. But Eric wants plain, raw wood, so his bat is just wrapped in a paper sleeve and boxed, along with 11 other model C271's. Soon, a box of one dozen bats is ready to be shipped to Eric.

Batter Up

The bats are sent to the Reds clubhouse at Riverfront Stadium in Cincinnati, Ohio. When Eric gets to the clubhouse the next day, the new shipment of bats is waiting for him. Eric receives about eight dozen (96) bats each season, but he only uses about two dozen. The extras are given away by the team, or just stay in Eric's bat bags, waiting to be used. To be on the safe side, Eric will usually take seven bats when he goes on a 14-game road trip.

No matter how many bats Eric has, he loves to check out each new shipment, because no two bats are ever *exactly* alike. He picks up a bat and checks the grain. The bat looks good. He feels the handle to see if it is thin enough. Then he swings it a few times to check the weight. Finally, he takes some cuts with it in batting practice.

Eric has found his new bat. He writes his number, 44, on the handle so the batboys will know it's his. Eric doesn't do much else to his bat. Some players rub their bats with a bone to make them harder, or clean them with rubbing alcohol, or put pine tar on the handles to make them sticky. Some players even talk to their bats!

Some players are superstitious. They believe that each bat can produce only a certain number of hits. Eric doesn't believe that. "I don't think that when they make bats they put 25 or 30 hits in them and then the bats will disintegrate," he says. "The bat won't come up and say, 'Look, dude, I have only two more hits in me.'" Even so, when Eric gets in a hitting slump, he might change bats.

Game time is approaching. Soon Eric will take his new C271 to the plate for its first official at-bat.

How many hits and homers does this bat have in it? There's no telling!

In the other articles in this chapter, you can discover what people have believed about trees, and what they've crafted out of the wood. It seems only fair—ecologically and otherwise—to include a piece about where it all begins.

Let's Plant a Tree

By Aileen Fisher

ALL: It's time to plant a tree, a tree.
What shall it be? What shall it be?
1ST: Let's plant a pine—we can't go wrong:
a pine is green the whole year long.
2ND: Let's plant a maple—more than one!
to shade us from the summer sun.
3RD: Let's plant a cherry—you know why:
There's nothing like a cherry pie!
4TH: Let's plant an elm, the tree of grace,
where robins find a nesting place.
5TH: Let's plant an apple—not too small,
with flowers in spring and fruit in fall.
6TH: Let's plant a fir—so it can be
a lighted outdoor Christmas tree.
7TH: Let's plant a birch, an oak, a beech,
there's something extra-nice in each.

ALL: It's time to plant a tree, a tree.
What shall it be? What shall it be?
It doesn't seem to matter much—
they all have special charms and such
in winter, summer, spring or fall.
Let's plant a . . .
look, let's plant them ALL!

5

CRAFT AND CRAFTINESS

In this article, you'll learn how to transform aluminum foil from your family's kitchen into gold. (Just kidding.) The ancient science of alchemy involved far more than simple get-rich-quick schemes. Benjamin Kilborne sheds some light on this most elusive of recipes—of changing base metals such as lead into gold.

Alchemy: Golden Heart of the Matter

By Benjamin Kilborne

Whether we think of the legend of the ancient King Midas, whose touch turned everything to gold, the goose that laid the golden egg, or the bars of gold worth billions of dollars stored in Fort Knox, gold has long been a source of economic, religious, and magical power. Dreams of making gold, or of transforming more ordinary metals such as tin or copper into gold, gave rise to the science of alchemy.

From the twelfth to about the eighteenth century, alchemists had three goals, often related to one another. Besides trying to change lesser metals into valuable metals like gold, they sought to cure illnesses with special potions (curative drinks) and to find the secret for mixing an elixir, or extract, that would make anyone who drank it young again.

Working toward these goals, alchemists sought to understand which elements create and maintain human and animal life. The search for these basic elements, the building blocks of matter, did not begin with the alchemists, however. Philosophers such as the ancient Greek thinker Aristotle believed that all nature could be explained in terms of four primary elements: earth, air, water, and fire. Alchemists took up Aristotle's ideas, experimenting with transforming metals, mixing ingredients in secret recipes in the hope of changing "impure" metals such as tin into "pure" metals such as gold.

To the alchemists, gold was not just a metal. They believed that it was indeed the purest form of matter and symbolized the secret of eternal life. For them gold, the heart and soul of matter, was the key to understanding the natural world and what lay behind it. But their ideas about the purity of gold also were religious and metaphysical (beyond the knowledge of the physical world).

As the soul animated the human body, the alchemists believed, so gold animated natural bodies such as the earth and the planets. By discovering the secrets of gold, the alchemists thought that they could grasp the secrets of everlasting life. Because gold neither corrodes nor loses its glitter over time, it became the symbol of a body that never changes and lives forever without aging.

According to one story, alchemy was founded by the god known to the Egyptians as Thoth, to the Greeks as Hermes, and to the Romans as Mercury. An important collection of early writings on religion and philosophy, the *Hermetica*, was filled with alchemical symbols uniting things both large and small and using the same symbol for the sun and gold. Later, alchemists became known as people who practiced the "Hermetic" art. They sealed their vessels with the seal of Hermes, from which we get the phrase "hermetically sealed," meaning tightly sealed.

Alchemists believed that the earth incubated elements to make gold, just as a chicken incubates an egg. All they needed to make gold, then, was the secret of what happens inside the earth. A Chinese prince of the early fifteenth century applied this idea logically and had a hen sit on an eggshell filled with cinnabar (a red mineral). He thought that the cinnabar would change to gold, given the right conditions. Whether in China, India, Egypt, or Greece, alchemists everywhere jealously guarded the secrets of their art.

The link between knowing how things changed and knowing the secret of living forever gave alchemy strong religious ties. In ancient Greece, it developed together with Hermeticism, and in China, it accompanied the beliefs of Taoism. In ancient India, where one text explains that "gold is immortality," alchemy evolved together with yoga. Further west in Asia it was linked with Islamic doctrines, and in Europe, during medieval and Renaissance times, it was linked with Christian ideas. Because they claimed to understand the secrets of nature independently from orthodox (officially accepted) Christian beliefs, alchemists in Europe were

This engraving, from a drawing by the great 16th-century artist Peter Brueghel, is a strong comment on the folly of alchemy. The alchemist (left) tries in vain to make gold, his wife (center) turns out her empty purse, and the children (top center) search the empty cupboard for food. The family's future appears at upper right, where they are received at the poorhouse.

sometimes believed to be servants of Satan, the Devil. In Genesis, the first chapter of the Bible, the fallen angels, or devils, whom God threw out of heaven taught the art of alchemy to the women they married.

In the latter part of the sixteenth century, alchemy took a new turn when the famous Swiss physician and alchemist Paracelsus declared that the true object of alchemy was not to transform lesser metals into gold but to prepare effective medicines to cure sick people. Paracelsus thought that the process of creation was no more than a chemical process. In his view, God was a divine chemist. Out of his work and that of alchemists before him grew what we know today as the science of chemistry, which deals with identifying and isolating the elements of matter and analyzing how they are combined and transformed. Religious and scientific, alchemy remains an important part of the world's history.

That sand can be made into glass seems more industrious than changing lead into gold. The conversation between father and son here is fictional, but the rest of the story is true. Sand-blowing is also ancient with its origins in myth. And glassmaking—more of a miracle than an industry—is part of U. S. history and spirit.

America's First Industry

By Lee Beasley

The southern New Jersey sky lightened, announcing the dawn on a cool September morning in 1739. Twelve-year-old Richard Wistar followed his father, Caspar, out of Johannes Wentzel's house. Caspar had arrived yesterday from their home in Philadelphia to inspect progress at his new glasshouse and to join Richard in glass-blowing lessons with Wentzel.

Two years ago, Caspar had announced his plans to start a glasshouse. Last spring, four master glass blowers, including Wentzel, had come to New Jersey from Germany to work for him. Immediately they had started constructing the buildings for the glassworks, then the furnace, ovens, and equipment. During the summer, Richard, as part of the crew, had carried and stacked wood for the drying ovens; shoveled sand into bins; raked out and stored ashes in other bins; dug and hauled clay for pots that would hold the melting sand mixture; and trundled bricks for the furnace and annealing ovens.

Now he and his father were entering the finished glassworks, housed in a large, high-ceilinged building. They heard the muffled roar of the fire in the cone-shaped furnace and were enveloped by the heat and smell of wood in the drying ovens.

Wentzel waved them over to two benches near the furnace. As the Wistars sat down, Wentzel announced, "We'll blow a bottle first." He showed them how to handle the blowpipe.

Richard soon found that blowing glass was much more difficult than it looked. Wentzel's skills, developed over years of working with molten glass, made his maneuvers look easy, but by afternoon, Richard and his father knew that bringing the four artisans from Germany had been a wise investment.

Before dark, as Richard and his father walked down to Alloway Creek for a swim, Richard asked, "Is ours the first glassworks in the colonies?"

"No," Caspar replied. "In 1608, several Jamestown settlers built a glassworks and operated it for a year or two. This was

America's first industry, and its bottles were shipped back to London. Some other Jamestown settlers tried to operate the works again in 1621, but it failed."

"What happened?" Richard asked.

"The settlers had many problems—hostile Indians, illnesses, poor food," Caspar said. "Many starved during the hard winters."

"During the last century," he went on, "a few glasshouses started in Salem of Massachusetts colony, in New Amsterdam,* and in Philadelphia. None was successful."

"What made them quit?"

"They faced two big problems," Caspar said. "They set up glasshouses without enough funds to operate such an expensive undertaking, and they had trouble keeping skilled workers. We are different because we have the profits from our button and iron businesses and because of our partnership with Johannes and the other three glass blowers. If we make money, so do they. If not, we all lose."

"Why did you decide to start a glasshouse?" Richard asked.

"The colonies are growing. New businesses and homes need window glass and bottles and pitchers for containers. Imported glass can't meet the demand, and it is very expensive. Many people make do with oiled paper over their window openings and earthen, pewter, or wood containers for food and liquids."

His father stopped, then continued in a softer tone. "Besides, glass fascinates me.

*This Dutch colony became New York City.

America's first glasshouse, at Jamestown, probably looked much like this, with three rounded ovens for melting glass.

We take sand and a few other ingredients from the earth. By heating and working with them, we create useful and beautiful objects."

Richard recalled one evening when the family had been sitting at the dinner table. His father had been entranced by his wineglass, slowly turning it in the light, admiring its sparkle. Richard swallowed. For the first time, his father had talked to him as to another adult. He would always remember this day.

During the following years, the Wistar businesses flourished. After his father died in 1752, Richard continued to manage them successfully.

In 1763, he heard that German-born Henry Stiegel had set up a successful glasshouse at Elizabeth Furnace, west of Philadelphia. Some years later, Richard learned that Stiegel had expanded his operation with two more furnaces at Manheim, Pennsylvania. By 1774, due to the troubled times and Stiegel's finances, his glassworks had failed, and he had been sent to debtor's prison.

The hard times of the Revolutionary War damaged the Wistar businesses, too. In 1780, Richard closed his glassworks. He died the following year. Nevertheless, Caspar and Richard Wistar's success had given glassmaking its start as a major American industry.

People could write letters in the sand, but before they began to use the papyrus plant and parchment (which doesn't exactly grow on trees) they couldn't mail those letters. And the postage on stone tablets may have been exorbitant. In fact, if you were an ancient child who wanted to know what a friend was up to, you'd probably have to visit his family's home to read their cave paintings.

Papyrus and Parchment

For thousands of years, stones, rocks, dirt, and tree trunks provided workable, albeit rough, surfaces on which humans could visually express their thoughts and desires. The Stone Age paintings discovered in caves in southern France, the enormous designs on the plains of Peru in South America, and the numerous inscriptions found in and on temples throughout the Mediterranean world all point to the need that every human being has to communicate. Yet words must be seen and read; otherwise, they have no true value.

In time, portable writing materials—clay tablets, wax tablets, small stones, and even animal skins—came into use. All, however, had disadvantages—e.g., they broke easily, or they were very heavy. Gradually, people discovered the papyrus plant and the fact that paper could be made from its inner stem. The earliest extant specimen—a blank papyrus roll found in an Egyptian tomb—dates to c. 3000 B.C.

Papyrus

As the centuries passed, the art of making paper from papyrus was perfected, and it became the standard writing material in ancient times. The Roman naturalist Pliny the Elder (A.D. 23/24–79) included a detailed description of the process used to manufac-

Collecting and Preparing the Papyrus Plant for Making Paper (From a tomb at Thebes, Egypt, c. 1500 B.C.)

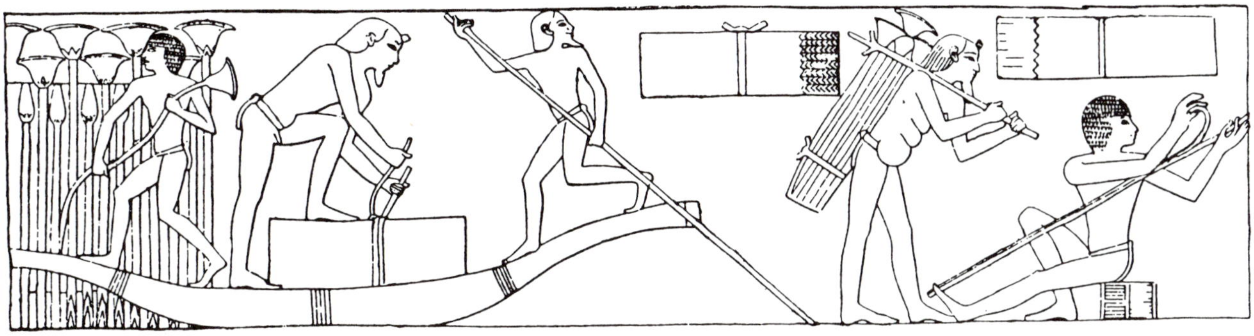

Papyrus Plants Along the Nile

ture paper in his *Natural History*, xiii, 74–82.

The papyrus plant, which used to grow in abundance in Egypt, especially around the delta of the Nile River, reaches a height of ten to fifteen feet. Its triangular, smooth-stemmed reed has a tufted plume of leaves and flowers at the top. However, only the stem was used to make paper from papyrus.

Inside the outer rind are approximately twenty concentric layers of very light membranes (similar in texture to onion skins). These were separated by using a needle. The innermost layers were the best; the outermost layer was quite coarse, unsuitable for paper, and used to make rope. The strips were laid side by side, vertically, on a slightly dampened flat surface until the desired width was obtained. The width of each strip varied considerably. Atop the vertical layer came a second layer of papyrus strips, at right angles to the first—i.e., arranged horizontally. This "sheet" of papyrus was then placed in a press to "bond" the two layers together. After sufficient time had passed, the papyrus was removed, beaten with a mallet, and rubbed with an ivory tool, a shell, or a pumice stone to produce a smooth, unwrinkled polished effect.

Single sheets were fastened together using a type of artificial paste and then assembled into a roll, which is believed to have consisted of twenty sheets. The seams were so well formed that they were almost unnoticeable.

Papyrus sheets are extremely durable and flexible, as is evidenced by several recent twentieth-century discoveries of papyrus rolls. These sheets, although used often at the time they were made and then rolled up for centuries, can still be rolled and unrolled easily.

Parchment

Papyrus was so popular and in such great demand in ancient times that it was said that Egyptian rulers could and did fund programs and projects with papyrus revenues. As the decades passed, however, another type of paper, parchment, became widely used.

According to the ancients, parchment appeared as the result of a rivalry between the rulers of Egypt, the Ptolemies, and the rulers of Pergamum in Asia Minor (present-day Turkey), the Attalids. According to the story, when Egypt realized that Pergamum planned to establish a library that would rival the famed library at Alexandria in Egypt, the Ptolemies ordered all shipments of papyrus to Pergamum stopped. This action so infuriated King Eumenus II (197–159 B.C.) of Pergamum that he resolved to retaliate not with force but with ingenuity. His people invented a type of paper that the Romans called *pergamena* (after the city of its origin). This paper, known to us as parchment, a corrupted form of pergamena, soon became more widely used than papyrus. Until recently, diplomas and various types of legal documents were all written on parchment.

To make this material, the people of Pergamum used the skins of sheep and goats. Each skin was carefully washed and left to soak in a vat of pure water for approximately twenty-four hours. The skin was then placed in another vat filled with a mixture of water and fresh lime. The skin remained in this second vat for a period of eight to fifteen days. Workers then scraped the skin with sharp instruments to remove the coarse hair. Often a second soaking in a lime solution followed the scraping. Again workers scraped and rubbed the skin. To produce the finest parchment, chalk was often sprinkled on the skin, which was then rubbed and polished with pumice stones. Lastly, the skin was allowed to dry, often by being placed or stretched on a frame.

Within a few centuries parchment, not papyrus, had become the preferred paper of the ancient world.

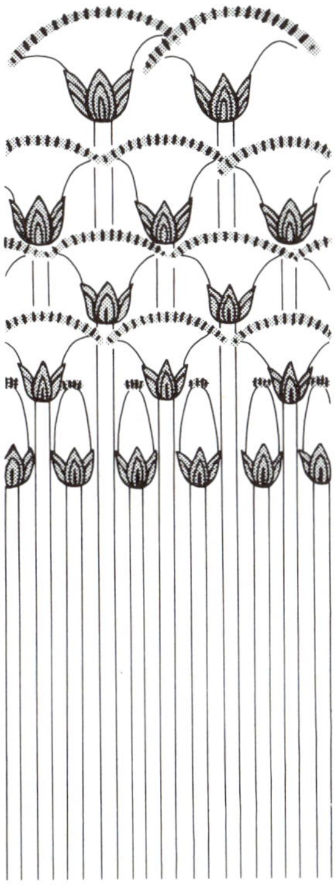

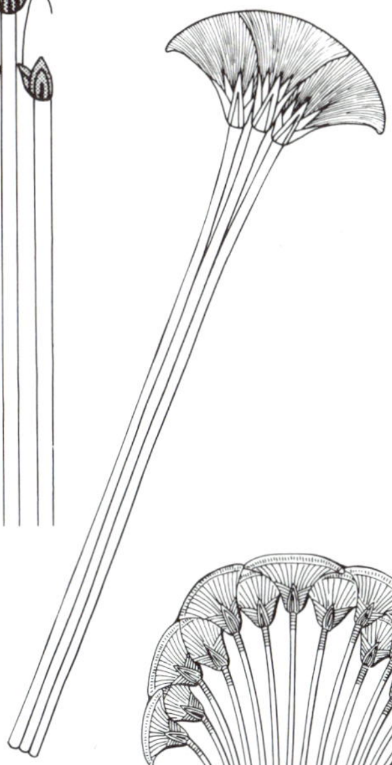

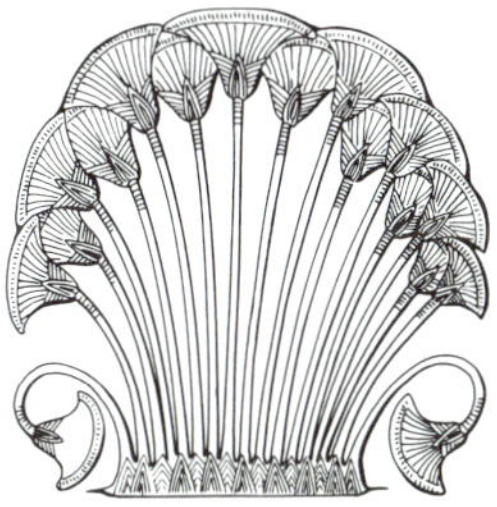

Neatly Folded Private Letters Written on Papyrus; Discovered in the Late 1800s in Egypt

It's too easy for us to believe that older civilizations somehow knew less than we do. But knowledge is relative—and you'll be astonished by the array of processes the ancients invented and used to make their lives easier.

What the Ancients Used

Dry Cleaning

The ancients, especially the Egyptians and Romans, developed a thorough and effective method of cleaning their clothes that used water mixed with special herbs, plants, and urine. (N.B. The urine was collected in vessels placed on street corners and then allowed to decompose before it was used.)

First, the entire cloth was placed (or portions were dipped) into vessels containing the cleansing liquid. Then the cleaners used mallets and wooden sticks to beat the cloth. Roman wall paintings show cleaners using their hands and actually stepping into the vessels to pound the cloth with their feet. The wet, washed cloth was allowed to dry before being rinsed again and then brushed with special tools (made of teasel, burs, thistles, or hedgehog prickles) to raise the nap.

To bleach the cloth, the garment was placed over a wicker frame, inside of which was a pan or pot filled with burning sulfur. Since this process did not bleach evenly, the ancients rubbed the material with white or colored earth, depending on the color of the cloth. Another brushing followed, then the uneven fibers and threads were cut from the garment. Finally, the cloth was pressed between two boards worked by screws.

Publishing

The invention of printing about A.D. 1440 signaled the end of the tedious recopying of every letter on every page of a book, text, speech, or law—a process that required hours of a person's time and days to complete. But there had been a time, centuries earlier, when book publishing went at a relatively rapid pace.

The first century B.C. saw the first great rise in the number of slaves in Rome. As conquest followed conquest, more slaves were sent to Rome. Since many of them were well educated, they became teachers and professionals, although socially they remained slaves.

Educated Romans and others saw in these slaves a means to reprint great numbers of books, speeches, and decrees. The process was as follows. Fifty, maybe even

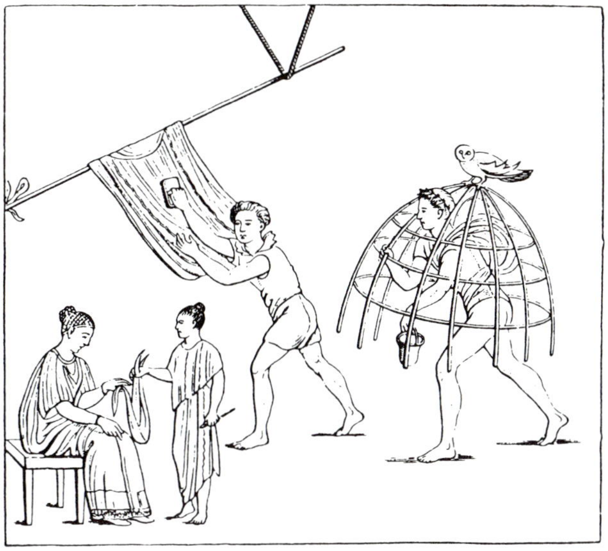

Four people prepare and clean clothes at the fuller's shop.

one hundred, of these educated slaves would sit in a room. A reader would stand before them and dictate a book, page by page. If more than one room or area was used and more readers were available, a book could be divided into sections, and in a relatively short period of time, as many copies as there were slaves would be ready for distribution.

Refrigeration

The Greeks and Romans dug large pits and covered them with grass, chaff, earth, manure, tree branches, and other similar substances that do not conduct heat. Then they collected snow from the mountains, pressed it compactly together, and placed it inside the pit as a lining. Sometimes the snow was wrapped in thick cloths as a further measure against its melting. Ancient sources credit the Roman emperor Nero (A.D. 54–68) with inventing the "cooler." One day a shipment of produce packed in snow came to Rome from the north. Nero observed that the contents were quite cool as a result of having been next to the snow, not mixed with it. He applied the same principle to drinks. Consequently, water and wine no longer needed to be mixed with snow to keep them cool. A glass or container filled with liquid needed only to be placed in the snow to keep the contents cold.

Telegraphy

Very early in human history, people learned to flash fire signals to members of other tribes. Through the centuries, many ingenious systems of telegraphy have been devised. Polybius, a second century B.C.

Scribe, Bookcase, and Writing Implements (This relief dates from the Later Empire, perhaps the 5th century A.D.)

Greek historian, wrote about the system he invented.

Provide each tribe or participant with ten torches. Divide the torches into two groups of five each. Divide the twenty-four letters of the Greek alphabet into four groups of five letters each and one group of four letters. Let the five torches in one group represent the five groups of Greek letters. Let each of the five torches in the other group represent a specific Greek letter from its group.

To flash a message, have the person on duty use the following rules to spell out each word. First, raise the required number of torches in the first set of five to indicate the group to which a particular letter belongs. Then have him raise the required number of torches in the other set to indicate the specific letter within the group.

This system was accurate but tedious and required hours to spell out a message of considerable length.

"Crafts" is such a deceptive word—these colonial women weren't gluing together popsicle sticks. People may have discovered paper-making, but other conveniences didn't exist. A day in the life of a colonial wife (and her children) was just one long chore.

Housewifely Crafts

by Terry Ren Rugno

By the mid-1700s, wealthy families in Colonial America, especially in the larger towns, could buy most of the household goods they needed. They sent for them from England or bought goods from local merchants or craftsmen. But many families had little money, and people in rural areas did not always have a ready source of supplies. Just as Colonial families had done since the early 1600s, these families made what they needed, including everything from breads and jams to candles and bed quilts.

Colonial housewives worked long hours to provide food, clothing, and comfort. Preparing food for the dinner table was a daily challenge. As part of that work, the Colonial housewife turned hogs into sausages, milk into golden cheese, fruit into jam and cider, and herbs into medicine. Such preserved foodstuffs made winter survival possible.

Providing the home with candlelight was difficult, unpleasant work. All through the year, the family saved every scrap of animal fat. For several days in the fall, this fat, called tallow, was boiled with water and the impurities were skimmed off the top until the tallow was clear.

Early on the day set aside for candle dipping, large kettles were filled with clear tallow and water. Two long poles were laid across chair backs with candle rods placed across them like ladder rungs. Several strings were looped over each rod at intervals, with the ends twisted to form candlewicks.

The woman dipped a rod of wicks into the kettle, then hung it back on the poles. Each time the tallow cooled and hardened, she dipped the wicks again, adding layers of tallow until the candles became fat enough. A good worker might make two hundred candles in a day. Waxy bayberries could be used to produce special candles with a pleasant scent.

The family's clothes were made from wool and flax. In the spring, the sheep's winter coat was clipped, picked clean of knots and trash, scrubbed, and sometimes dyed. Tree bark, roots, flowers, nuts, and berries supplied rich, colorful dyes. Dyes also could be purchased.

The fleece was then greased to prepare it for carding, a process in which the wool was combed back and forth between two wire-tooth brushes, mixed, and fluffed to form a roll of soft wool. The woman then set the

A self-reliant Colonial family might have made its own cloth—the wife spinning and the husband weaving. In this print, one son weaves a mat out of rushes (the stems of a marsh plant).

spinning wheel in motion and held the roll to the turning spindle. Walking backward, she drew the wool out into yarn. Then stepping forward, she allowed the yarn to wind onto the spindle. Later wound onto a hand reel, or niddy-noddy, the yarn was measured off into skeins. A good day's work, producing six skeins of yarn, meant more than twenty miles of walking.

The preparation of flax was far more complicated, requiring about twenty dirty, tiring steps before the fibers could be spun. The smaller, lighter flax wheel was a foot wheel, operated while the woman was seated.

Both wheels produced thread for weaving. Some cloth may have been made on the family's huge homemade loom. Men usually did the weaving, and professional craftsmen, often traveling weavers, would weave the family's linen thread into fine cloth for light clothing, sheets, and napkins. Warm clothing and blankets were made from heavier wool cloth. The two types of thread were combined to make linsey-woolsey, a common fabric that was strong and warm but very scratchy. Wool yarn also was knit into warm stockings and mittens, often using complicated patterns and stitches.

From earliest times, Colonial women decorated their creations with fancy-work. They netted fringes for edging curtains, coverlets, and petticoats and embroidered gowns, bed hangings, and curtains. Embroidery on netting, or tambour work, produced lace for collars and infants' clothing. To make quilts, thrifty housewives saved scraps of material and pieced them together in beautiful, complicated patterns.

All these activities resulted in a heavy workload for the Colonial housewife. Sometimes two women with the same task at hand—for example, making soap—would do the work together, first at one home, then at the other. They called this change-work. When the work required many hands, neighbors gathered for a bee. Southern plantations were too far apart for such neighborliness, but women elsewhere held bees for quilting, sewing, knitting, and spinning.

By the mid-1700s, when fabric was commonly imported from England, spinning was no longer done in so many homes. Before and during the Revolution, however, housewives turned to their spinning wheels as part of their protest against England (see article on page 82). Often a woman would strap her wheel behind her saddle and, carrying her baby, ride to a neighbor's spinning circle.

Quilting bees were the most popular. When a woman finished her patchwork, she invited ten or twelve neighbors in to help her put the quilt together. They stacked the quilt back, several layers of soft stuffing, and the patchwork top. Then they sewed the edges together and stretched the quilt across a wooden frame. Finally, they sewed the layers together while stitching a decorative design on the quilt surface.

For many years, craft know-how was handed down from generation to generation. Girls learned embroidery stitches by sewing samplers. They learned to knit and sew in the dame schools, and some girls were bound out to a neighbor to learn spinning or weaving. But most learned the skills from mothers, grandmothers, and aunts. Even on southern plantations, the mistress taught her daughter these skills to prepare her to supervise the work of the slaves.

In time, many housewifely skills were taken over by craftsmen. Family members still spun the wool, but the wool was carded by machines at the mill. And it was often the traveling weaver who wove the cloth. Tailors visited households to make, or make over, clothes for the family and servants. The candle maker brought his own metal candle molds, but the family still had to save the fat for him and the traveling soap maker.

There may be some skeptics among you who won't believe that two crafty women could triumph so easily over the bad guy in this tale, set in the mountains near a gold mine. And you may be right. But the lively language makes the story worth a gander—and then, decide on the outcome yourself.

Strawberry Pink Yarn

By Theo E. Gilchrist

There were three of them in that mountain cabin home. Two tiny ladies, Betts and Em, with skin like pine bark. Hair white as mountain snow. Eyes blue as the streams. The third was Gabrielle, their frisky black goat. She gave them milk and friendship.

Betts toted the wood and water. Em puttered with fire and food. A small garden grew beets and onions, greens and potatoes.

In early summer they followed the mountain sheep. Em, with stiff legs but sharp eyes, could spot from far off the clumps of wool shed by the sheep and caught in the thorns and bushes. Betts, with nimble legs, ran over the slopes gathering up the wads and fibers by the sackful. Em washed the wool, combed it, and spun it into yarn—yards and yards of yarn.

With her special vision Em saw colors. She saw the blossoms, the roots, the bark, and the berries she knew could make dyes for the yarn. Betts spent the best of her time exploring the crevices, poking in potholes, digging in the bends of streams and the river looking for stray nuggets of gold. At the same time, she fetched the plants and berries Em wanted. In a big wooden tub, Em steeped and stirred, steeped and stirred, until the color was right for the yarn.

Gabrielle nibbled greens and gave milk. They had no other needs. They were happy.

Until one day, far below in the green valley, the old judge shook his gray head. "Only the mountains, the river, and the boarded-up mine be older than Em and Betts," he said to the stranger. "Sisters they say. Been living up there in that cabin beyond anyone's memory." He paused. "Why, stranger? You kin or something?"

The heavy stranger muttered. "Good old Em and Betts." His flabby hand tightened its hold on his walking stick. "Kin is what I am. I'm aiming to make a call." He turned and spat and stumbled up the path.

"Ha," he mumbled. "Two old hags. Right in the shadow of the Long-Ago Mine. Alone. I know they're hoarding gold. I know I'm getting my share. After all, ain't we kin?" His glinty eyes sought out the white curl of smoke marking the cabin.

Betts was helping Em wind the yarn into a huge ball.

"Wild strawberry pink! This is the biggest and prettiest yet, Betts."

"Heaviest, too. Who'd ever guess there's gold inside these yarn balls."

Em smiled. "Just look at that pile." The balls were stacked in a huge reed basket. They reached halfway up the wall, with the strawberry pink teetering on top.

"Onion rust, beet purple, elderberry blue, laurel tan, and lichen green. Oh, the wonder of it all, Betts."

"The weight of it all, Em."

"The gifts of nature, Betts."

"Along with my working legs, Em."

"If you ever have a need, Betts, I can knit hundreds of sweaters to sell."

"If *you* ever have a need, Em, I'll buy them from you with all that gold."

Their laughter rang down the mountainside.

Outside Gabrielle pawed the ground nervously. Then the sisters heard. Twigs snapping. Stones tumbling. Cursing. Grunting. Wheezing.

"Now, who . . . ?" Betts asked as the cabin door swung open.

The man stumbled inside. "Your dear Cousin Jake is who." The smell of his sweat filled the room.

"Cousin Jake?" questioned Betts.

"Well . . . are you Hiram's boy?" Em asked.

"Yup, that's me. Old Hiram's boy."

Em looked surprised and said, "You seem tired. Would you like a cup of goat's milk?"

"No, I don't like goat anything." Gabrielle snorted from the doorway. "You got water?"

"There's a spring out back. Help yourself," said Em.

As he left the cabin Betts whispered, "Cousin Jake? More likely Cousin Fake. And who's Hiram?"

Em smiled, "Beats me. Never heard of him."

"He's a varmint," said Betts. "I ought to take that strawberry pink ball and pound his head."

Em shook her finger. "He's got to go. But it wouldn't be fit to harm a lazy hulk like him. We have to gentle him away."

"I'll thing of something," Betts said.

At the spring Jake kneeled down and cupped his hands. Gabrielle, who followed, eyed the monstrous rear end in front of her. She lowered her head and, with a rush, butted Jake flat into the water. He stumbled to his feet and kicked at her, but the nimble goat trotted out of the way.

Dripping wet, Jake sloshed back to the cabin, grumbling to himself.

"Some mean goat you got here! Ought to get rid of it."

Betts choked back her laughter. "Gabrielle is family to us. She gives us milk and keeps us company."

"You got me now. And besides, I aim to protect you."

"From what?"

"Well, little cousins, you know someone's bound to think you got gold here."

"Where?"

"You must have a basement or some hiding place." His eyes searched the cabin.

"We've no such thing," Em said. "But it's getting dark now. You better fetch a bucket of water and have a bowl of potato soup. There's cheese and berries, too."

Jake lugged in the water puffing and coughing.

"Here's a blanket," Betts said. "When you're through eating, you can make yourself cozy in the shed with Gabrielle." Jake looked fearful. Gabrielle snorted.

Night settled in quiet—for a while. Then

from the shed: *BUMP! CRASH! CRACK! THUMP! WHACK!*

Watching from their little window, the sisters saw Jake come flying out, trailing his blanket. He ran and slumped to the ground under the pines where he slept until the next afternoon. When he awoke, he came stumbling into the cabin, puffing and coughing, carrying a bucket of water.

"Here's some water," he said to Em. "But don't ask for more. Too heavy."

"Well, thank you, Cousin. Will you milk Gabrielle?"

"That goat? Never!"

"How about digging up potatoes?"

"Ground's too hard. Where's Cousin Betts?"

"She went down the mountain real early. Thought a hard-working man like you might need meat."

"What's she using for money? Gold?"

Em laughed. "Gold? How silly! She trades balls of my colored yarn."

"Yah, I see that pile," Jake said, walking toward the yarn.

"Don't touch," Em ordered. "Yarn ain't worth much with dirty hand smears on it."

Jake backed away and sat down just as Betts burst into the room.

"You're right, Cousin Jake. Look here now." She held out a tiny lump of gold. "It was all I could get without tools."

Jake seized the nugget. His eyes flashed. "Where'd you find it?"

"Far, far down the mountain."

"Can you find the place again?" Jake asked.

"I marked the trail with knots of strawberry pink yarn tied to bushes and trees. I'm going back tomorrow. But, Em, since I got us no meat, we'll climb up a ways and fetch some berries."

Em hesitated. Betts put an arm about her waist. "I'll help you up the rough places. Come, Gabrielle. Cousin Jake?"

"Nope, I need rest."

Gabrielle snorted, and the three started up a path in back of the cabin. Em hobbled along painfully. "Betts, you out of your mind?"

"We'll see. Come on, Em. It's just a little way to Lookout Rock. We can watch the cabin without being seen."

They were there shortly. Betts helped Em up. Gabrielle followed. They crouched down and peeked over the edge. All was quiet below.

"He's taking his rest," Em said.

Betts shook her head. "His greed will give him strength. You watch."

Soon the three pairs of eyes saw the cabin door open. Out came Cousin Jake carrying a pick and a gold pan. He looked about cautiously and then started at a half run. He snatched the first yarn tie off the pine branch and started down the trail.

"See, he's taking my markers, making sure I won't follow," Betts said.

"But he's taking your tools, too!"

"The pan has holes, and the pick handle's split. I hid my good ones away."

"You think he'll come back?"

"Never. He'll be too worn out falling down cliffs, fighting river rapids, snaking his way through the canyon where I pitched the last of the yarn. Besides, he's destroying the trail."

"What a shame!" Em exclaimed.

"Shame? Em, I gentled him away like you said and even gave him a wee gold nugget."

"But we didn't kiss dear Cousin Jake good-bye. That's the shame."

Gabrielle nuzzled them both and leaped high into the air.

6

MASTERY OR WHO'S RUNNING THE SHOW?

You've probably had some work experience—doing odd jobs around the house, taking care of your little brothers and sisters, or running errands for neighbors. Imagine, instead, being apprenticed to a local manufacturer and serving him for several years. Not so long ago, that's just how many young people learned a trade. And, maybe later on, those former apprentices would take on apprentices themselves.

The Apprentice System

By Robert D. San Souci

Based on the English model, the apprentice system trained most boys and some girls in a craft that would become their livelihood. At about age fourteen, a youngster was bound over to a master craftsman. A written contract between the child's parents and the master, called an indenture, usually promised that the child would serve the master for seven years, although the length of time could vary. In return, the master promised to teach the new apprentice his trade. The master also was obliged to teach the youngster how to read and write or to allow him to attend evening school to acquire such learning.

The everyday life of the trainee was not easy. Imagine, for example, the apprentice pewterer beginning his day before sunup, stoking the fire in the forge. He might have had to coat the inside of the larger molds with a paste made of ocher, egg white, and vinegar to keep the molten pewter from sticking to them. He would then preheat the molds, baking on the paste and preparing them for the day's casting.

Assisting the master, he would hold the hinged mold shut with long handles while his teacher filled it with melted pewter. When the casting was withdrawn from the mold, the apprentice would help remove any extra bits of metal, fill in pits caused by air bubbles, and smooth the surface of the new plate or pot. He would run the treadle to turn the lathe while the master skimmed the casting to ensure smoothness. The apprentice would then burnish and polish the object. Other daily duties included cleaning the workplace.

When the shop was closed at day's end, the apprentice would eat, and then the master would teach him to read, write, and do sums. Or the master might send the boy to a privately run evening school where he would learn these basic skills as well as some others, such as bookkeeping.

Toward the end of the apprenticeship, the boy would submit an apprentice piece to his master. If this satisfied the master, the latter would sign off on the indenture, and the apprentice would become a journeyman, the next step to becoming a master craftsman. Given a "freedom suit" of new clothes by his master and often a set of tools appropriate to his trade, the fledgling journeyman would set out to find new work and continue his education in the craft.

Let's spell this out, even at the expense of being redundant: The falconer is the master, and the bird is his trainee. In the past and now, only the wealthy had time for what has been called "the sport of kings." Unless you have access to some crown jewels, or a thriving paper route, you may not be able to take it up yourself. But you can read more about it elsewhere; Jean Craighead George wrote of a contemporary hero who used this ancient means of hunting to survive in the wild in My Side of the Mountain.

Falconry

By Dean Amadon

In the sport of falconry, people use trained falcons to hunt other birds such as quail, doves, and wild ducks. Falcons are one kind of bird of prey; other kinds are hawks, eagles, and owls. Long ago, the Chinese and Persians found that birds of prey, which hunt for their food, can be trained to hunt food for humans. A falcon is caught in a net baited with a bird. Within a matter of weeks, the falconer can train it so that it can be released in the wild to pursue a quail or dove. It will then return to the falconer's fist, where he rewards it with bits of meat.

The peregrine falcon ("to peregrinate" means to wander far and wide), when trained, will climb and circle high in the sky. If the falconer or his dog causes a quail or duck to fly up, the falcon will plunge like an arrow and hit the prey, killing it instantly. Sometimes the falcon misses, and that also is part of the sport. The falcon has tiny bells on its legs to help the owner find it should it chase the prey out of sight. Nowadays a beeper like those carried by doctors may be used.

Other birds of prey also are used in hunting, and the term "falconry" is used for all sports of this nature. In central Asia, the Mongols train golden eagles to hunt foxes and wolves. The eagle flies after the fox or wolf, grabs it by the jaws, and holds it until the hunters and dogs run up to help. Short-winged hawks such as the goshawk (from gosling hawk) hunt rabbits and pheasants, and even the red-tailed hawk and the Harris' hawk can be trained to catch rabbits and squirrels. However, none of these birds is as thrilling to watch as a falcon, which hunts by soaring high in the sky and then swooping down on its prey in a spectacular dive.

Falconry is partly pageantry, partly the thrill of training and hunting, and partly a means of getting meat for the dinner table. In the old days, the difficulty and expense of getting and training falcons limited the sport to emperors and nobles. When Marco Polo made his famous trip to China in the 13th century, he found that the emperor Kublai Khan had hundreds of trained falcons and employed dozens of falconers. The emperor would be carried out to the field and recline on cushions as he watched the sport. In old England, the kind of bird that a person might own was defined by law according to rank, and the prized peregrine falcons and gyrfalcons, a related species of hawk, were reserved for royalty. Most prized of all were the pure white arctic gyrfalcons.

Today falconry is carried on chiefly in wide-open spaces such as the western United States and Canada, Pakistan, and Arabia.

Falconry is a time-consuming pursuit. Even after training, the birds need much attention and exercise to keep them healthy and in flying shape. Every time a valuable falcon is taken into the field, there is a chance that it will disappear, be shot by someone who dislikes all "chicken hawks," or be killed or disabled by another hawk or by flying into telephone wires.

Although falconers have done much to save birds of prey and to increase the public's appreciation of them, some people still oppose falconry. Morro Rock, a spectacular formation on the coast of California, was the site of one of the few remaining peregrine falcon eyries (nest ledges) along that coast. Although the nest was guarded day and night, two thieves climbed the cliff on a dark night and stole the young falcons.

Peregrine falcons nearly became extinct in the 1950s because they were poisoned by pesticides such as DDT. More have been bred in captivity by falconers and released, and now a few even nest on ledges of skyscrapers or on the girders underneath bridges such as the Verrazano Bridge in New York City.

The falcon in this portrait by 17th-century Dutch painter Aelbert Cuyp is a sign of high rank. In Europe, falconry became a sport among the noble classes.

People say leaders have that "certain something," meaning that they have an edge or strength we can't quite define. But it may not be true. The list below breaks down those qualities most leaders have or inspire in others. Take Destiny into your own hands! If you think you aren't cut out to be the president of your class, the school newspaper editor, or the head of the neighborhood club, think again.

Do You See Yourself as a Leader?

Are people really "born" leaders? No, says Warren Bennis, a professor at the University of Southern California's school of business.

"Learning to lead is a lot easier than most of us think it is, because each of us has the capacity for leadership," says Dr. Bennis, whose decade of research and interviews with prominent people led to the publication of his book, *On Becoming a Leader*.

Recently companies have shown more interest in developing leadership qualities in their employees. Training seminars teach employees that being a leader is a valued attribute in the workplace.

Dr. Bennis identifies six basic ingredients that characterize leaders. To see how you rate as a leader now—and potentially as a leader in the workplace—take a sheet of paper and list an example of your leadership for each category.

- *Vision*. Leaders have clear ideas, or goals, of what they want to accomplish, personally and professionally, and the strength to persist in the face of setbacks, even failures. What are your goals?

- *Passion*. Leaders love what they do and they love doing it. Leaders have an underlying passion for the promises of life, combined with a particular passion for a vocation, a profession, or a course of action. Their enthusiasm is contagious.

- *Integrity*. The essential parts of integrity are self-knowledge, honesty, and maturity.

- *Trust*. A leader elicits trust. This is the one quality that cannot be acquired; it must be earned.

- *Curiosity*. The leader wonders about everything and wants to learn as much as he or she can.

- *Daring*. The leader is willing to take risks, experiment, and try new things. Errors and failures don't discourage leaders, but give them a chance to learn and improve.

How do you score yourself on the leadership scale? Not as high as you'd like? Don't worry, Dr. Bennis advises.

"As countless deposed kings and hapless heirs to great fortunes can attest," he explains, "true leaders are not born, but made, and usually self-made. To become a leader, you must become yourself, become the maker of your own life."

What leadership boils down to is a strong sense of self that carries over into everything you do. Know and be true to yourself first, and your leadership ability may come forth more easily than expected.

Most people know about the Boston Tea Party, when American colonists were weary of British taxes. But there were other, less-famous revolts as these same colonists grew weary of British cloth, British candles—and the British themselves.

Tools of Political Rebellion

By Sharon M. Howard

Homespun clothing and hand-dipped candles seem unlikely weapons in a fight for independence. But with typical American ingenuity, these symbols of self-reliance were used to speak out against British laws that seemed unfair when Americans began the protests that led to the Revolutionary War.

Because candles were expensive and difficult to make, they were highly valued. In many homes, they were saved for Bible reading, school lessons, and other special occasions. On Christmas Eve, colonists placed candles in their windows, and at dusk each household lit them, creating a beautiful display of golden light. This simultaneous candle lighting was called an illumination. When wealthy or noble Englishmen visited the colonies, British officials would sometimes order an illumination in their honor. As such orders became more frequent, the thrifty colonists refused to cooperate. They were determined to keep illuminations for special occasions. Even today, a light in the window is a symbol of welcome.

British lawmakers were unhappy about another political protest that was taking place at that time. They had decided to raise taxes on many imported items, including fabric. But American craftsmen were becoming skilled and self-sufficient, and they could make their own fabric. Many decided not to buy any of the overtaxed British goods, and before long, wearing American homespun fabric was regarded as a badge of honor and a source of pride.

Judith may not have been in charge of her destiny, and, because she probably couldn't read or write in English, was unable to leave a record of her past. Unlike apprentices, who were indentured by some sort of mutual *agreement, slavery was an unjust imbalance of power. Judith's life was hard and probably sad, but this recreated story of her days in Williamsburg presents her composed dignity in the face of tremendous hardships.*

Judith: The Life of a Slave

By Cathleene Hellier and Brandon Miller

She was known simply as Judith, and what she felt or thought about her life as a slave in eighteenth-century Williamsburg, we will never know. Slaves made up half of Williamsburg's population, but none left a written record of their feelings about slavery.

Many families in Williamsburg owned slaves, but most owned only one or two. Wealthier families might have owned ten to fifteen slaves but seldom more than twenty. Slaves were an important part of the daily life and business of the Virginia capital, although they were often overlooked by historians because they left no written record.

Most slaves in Williamsburg worked as domestic servants or were trained as craftsmen. Many domestic slaves performed several tasks, including nursing, ironing, spinning, gardening, and sewing. Slaves who worked as craftsmen included carpenters, blacksmiths, shoemakers, and cabinetmakers, among others.

From what we can gather, Judith was William Prentis's family cook. As cook, her workdays were long and demanding. The kitchen where she worked was separate from the house, and the open fire made it very hot during the long Virginia summers. Judith rose early to prepare the fire and to cook the Prentis family's breakfast. As soon as breakfast was cleared away, she began the preparations for dinner, the largest meal of the day, served early in the afternoon. Dinner in a household like the Prentis's might have included two courses, including several kinds of meat, vegetables, relishes, beverages, and desserts. Judith also cleaned the many pots, spits, and kettles required to make such a meal. Happily for her, the leftovers from dinner were served for supper in the early evening.

Judith had little spare time to spend with her family. Because she was the cook, however, her children often received special treats that their mother saved from the Prentis's table. Her older daughters probably helped her in the kitchen on occasion.

Judith and her children lived above the kitchen, under the eaves. They slept and kept their few possessions there. The slave owners supplied their domestic slaves with simple clothing and bedding. Sometimes the slaves even wore hand-me-downs from the master's family. Domestic slaves often received tips from guests, and some slaves earned money by raising chickens for sale.

They could spend this money in the local stores, buying better clothing for special occasions or items to make their living quarters more comfortable.

Some slave children, including Judith's daughter Molly, went to special schools for blacks, an unusual opportunity for slaves in Colonial Virginia. One school, the Bray School, was founded by an English philanthropic (charitable) organization that listed Benjamin Franklin as a member. The school in Williamsburg opened in 1760. Students were taught to read the Bible, keep themselves clean and behave well, and speak distinctly. The founders hoped that pupils would attend the school for three years, but this rarely happened. When children were old enough to work, they were usually taken out of school.

Like slaves everywhere, Judith lived under a strict legal code designed to prevent slave uprisings. Blacks could not possess weapons or assemble except for public worship. (Church teaching enforced the idea that it was their duty to be obedient and patient.) Punishments for stealing or for resisting a white man included whipping, mutilation (ears or hands chopped off), and hanging. Yet slaves who committed a crime in which a person was not killed usually received a light sentence if it was their first offense. Even though laws were strict, they were not always strictly enforced. For example, some masters allowed their slaves to have guns for hunting.

Runaway slaves were returned to their masters. Runaways were often trying to visit family members who lived in other parts of the colony. Some ran away because they were trying to escape a particular master. The busy capital was a favorite hide-out for runaways, and it seems that Williamsburg slaves did a fairly good job of hiding fugitives.

The family life of a slave was uncertain.

If a master died or got into debt, some or all of his slaves might be sold. Sometimes the members of slave families were sold to different masters who lived far apart. Slaves must have feared these separations. When William Prentis died in 1765, he willed Judith and her three children to his teen-age daughter Elizabeth. When Elizabeth died unmarried in 1770, Judith and her children passed to Elizabeth's older brother John. By then, Judith had at least five children. John also inherited the family home in Williamsburg, and Judith and her children continued to live on the property.

During each of these upheavals in the Prentis family, Judith probably worried about the fate of her own family. Yet she had more cause to worry when John Prentis became very sick in 1775. John's wife was mentally ill and would not be able to manage the household if her husband died. When he did die, Judith was alarmed to learn that he had bequeathed only three of her children to his brother Joseph. Another daughter, Molly, was to be kept by John's family but hired out to work for others. Her work would provide money to help support John's widow. Finally, Judith learned that because the widow could not run a household, Judith would no longer be needed. She and her youngest son, Tom, were to be sold at auction. Her worst fears had come true; she and her children would be separated.

The slaves of Colonial Williamsburg had a big impact on the city's life. These men and women worked in almost every household, in the taverns, at the college, and in the craft shops. Overall, Williamsburg slaves were a trained and skilled group. Some even had a little education. But what a Williamsburg slave actually felt, feared, or hoped for, we can only imagine.

7

A COMMUNITY OF GOOD NEIGHBORS (AND BAD ONES!)

In regions of the U. S., a robin redbreast is the first sign of spring, but children in other parts of the world think otherwise. The Wheel on the School *by Meindert DeJong tells a charming fictional story of nesting storks, but Lillian Bason offers you the facts about storks and the rooftop neighborhoods they inhabit.*

The Good Luck Stork

By Lillian Bason

When winter snows begin to melt in Europe, kids start to watch the sky. They're searching for a bird with long wings, a long neck, and long legs trailing behind—the first *white stork* of spring.

For hundreds of years, people have watched for storks to return from their winter homes in Africa. Long ago when one was spotted, a town watchman would blow his trumpet to announce the good news. Even today, people think of the stork as a sign of warmer weather and good luck.

Many stories have been told about storks. The most famous is that storks pick up human babies in ponds as the birds fly to Europe. The storks carry the babies in their beaks, according to the story, and deliver them to families.

Another old story says storks once were people, perhaps because they have such long legs and look so wise. Some people used to say white storks turned into humans in winter. Then they became birds again in spring.

Family Time

The first storks to arrive in the spring are usually males. Right away, each male must find an old nest or start building a new one. The nest needs to be near meadows, marshes, or rivers. In these places, each male and his mate will be able to hunt for mice, frogs, fish, and insects.

Storks also seem to like living near people. They build their nests high in trees or on rooftops, chimneys, or church steeples. They usually return to the same place each year—even to the same nest.

If a stork uses an old nest, he always adds more sticks, grass, rags, and other things to it. An old nest may grow to be as big as a small car!

Female storks show up a week of so after the males arrive. That's when the racket starts! When a male and female meet, they tilt their heads back and click their bills—*ra-ta-ta-tat!* This clattering can be heard from far away. It's the storks' way of saying, "Hi! Who are you?"

Soon the storks mate and the female lays three to five large white eggs. For about a month, both parents take turns sitting on the eggs. Then the downy chicks hatch, tiny and helpless. But there is one thing they try to do from the start—clatter their bills!

Parents feed the young storks until they are about ten weeks old. During that time, the youngsters are hopping around the nest and exercising their wings. Soon they are flying and learning to hunt. By the end of the summer, they'll be ready for the trip south.

South for Winter

When summer is over, the storks gather in large groups. They wait until the time is right to begin their flight to Africa, their winter home.

In spring the storks arrived just a few at a time. But when they leave in the fall, they fly off in flocks.

Storks are expert fliers and gliders. When they fly over land, warm air currents carry them high into the sky. Then they glide slowly downward for miles until more warm air carries them up again. They hardly have to flap their wings as long as they fly over land.

But a great body of water—the Mediterranean Sea—lies between Europe and Africa. To get across it, some storks fly to a place called Gibraltar, where the sea is narrowest. Others go far around it by flying to the Middle East.

The storks' long journey is full of danger. They can die in hail storms. They may bump into tall buildings or get tangled in power lines. Storks are even shot or trapped in some countries.

But still, storks arrive in Africa by the thousands. As in Europe, people in some parts of southern Africa watch for storks. To these people, the return of the big birds is a sign that the rainy season is near.

Now it's vacation time for the storks. They don't have to build nests or take care of babies. Instead, they eat and eat and *eat* —mostly locusts. They eat so many of these big insects that some people in Africa call the white stork "the great locust bird."

People Problems

Even though thousands of white storks are still flying around, there aren't as many as there used to be. In Africa, the storks are finding fewer locusts to eat. People often poison these pesky insects and other animals that eat crops. So the storks go hungry, or they eat animals that have been poisoned. Then the storks can get sick and die too.

In Europe, some of the storks' best nesting areas have been ruined. People drained and filled marshes so they could build on the land. They covered meadows with roads and buildings too. As marshes and meadows disappeared, storks couldn't find enough food. And so they had to find new places to build their nests.

But many people are trying to help storks. They are learning not to shoot or trap these big birds. They're putting platforms on tall poles so the storks have plenty of places for nests. Most important, people are saving marshes and meadows so storks will have plenty of places to rest and find food.

With a little luck and a lot of help from people, storks will brighten the skies for many more seasons.

Ever had a day when nothing *goes right? Maybe there's a reason. Maybe it's the Kibosh. Maybe, like the folks of this seaside community, you think you can cancel your plans and avoid problems that way. And maybe you don't know the first thing about how to change bad luck into good times. Read on.*

The Kibosh

By Sarah Ellis

Everybody in the seaside town of Aberbog knew that it was going to be a bad day. Mary the Baker found out first. A whole batch of bread wouldn't rise, and a tray of currant buns came out of the oven as black and hard as pebbles on the beach. The apple pastries had double salt, and the scones had no salt at all. The cookies spread out all over the trays, the cream puffs didn't puff, and the cheese bread stuck to the pans. "Tarnation," said Mary. "I was going to take that cheese bread to the picnic, but that puts the kibosh on that."

Meanwhile Martin the Fiddler was sitting on his front steps looking at his fiddle in bewilderment. "What's the matter with you, then? Your flats are sharp and your sharps are flat and you sound like a midnight alley cat. I was thinking I might learn a new jig for the picnic, but that puts the kibosh on that."

Martin and Mary met later that morning at the office of the *Aberbog Daily Breeze* where they had wandered to get their newspapers. They found Betty Pringle covered with ink and in a terrible temper. "No paper today," she announced. "The dad-blamed press has eaten the dad-blamed paper." And sure enough, when they peered into the office, they saw ripped and ink-splattered sheets of paper all over the floor around a half-dismantled press. "I was going to print a big announcement for the picnic tomorrow," said Betty, "but that puts the kibosh on that."

Perkins and Snik, the fishermen, were wandering by and heard her. "Just what I was saying to Snik," said Perkins. "We went up to the river early this morning to get some trout for the picnic and we didn't get a single bite. So that puts the kibosh on that idea."

"What should we do?" asked Mary.

"Let's go and see Peter," said Betty. "He knows what's what."

Peter the Potter was just taking a set of bowls out of the kiln when the visitors arrived. Two bowls were broken. "Not my day," said Peter.

"It's not *anybody's* day," said Martin. And then they all described their troubles.

Peter listened carefully. "Oh yes," he said. "That will be the Kibosh. You'll never see him, and he doesn't visit very often, but when he does come, he's tickled pink when everything goes wrong."

"What can we do?" asked Snik.

"Let's have a think," said Peter.

The people of Aberbog are very good at ideas, so it didn't take them long to come up with a plan to get rid of the Kibosh. They decided that Betty (who was strong) and Martin (who owned a shovel) should dig a pit in the woods and trap the Kibosh.

They baited the trap with things that a Kibosh would like. Mary gave them a burnt pie and a lumpy pudding. Perkins and Snik contributed a pair of leaky rubber boots. Betty lent all her books with unhappy endings. They gathered itchy sweaters, rocks with no fossils in them, three-leaf clovers, bottles of cider that had turned to vinegar, and invitations to parties that had been canceled.

They waited the whole night through, sitting on beach chairs and drinking hot chocolate out of thermoses. But all they caught was one raccoon. And Perkins sprained his ankle rescuing it.

The next day it was clear that the Kibosh was still around. The sky was cloudy, people woke up with stuffy noses, babies grizzled, dogs snapped, the hens didn't lay, and there were no interesting packages in the mail. Everyone grumped down to the town square and frowned at one another.

"I think we should cancel the picnic," said Perkins.

"No point trying to have fun while that old Kibosh is still around," said Snik.

"Yes, let's just forget it," said the crowd.

"Wait a minute," said Peter. "I think we should have the picnic. If we can't trap that Kibosh, let's *scare* him away. Let's have such a good time that he'll get disgusted and go elsewhere."

The idea appealed to everyone, so plans were hatched. Betty went back to the print shop, cleaned up, and started to print a song sheet for everyone. Martin went home and tried a new tuning on his fiddle. Mary measured very carefully when she set about making a new batch of cheese buns. Everybody put on their most comfortable clothes. There was quiet humming in the pottery.

In the late afternoon the whole town gathered on the beach. There were fires and bright blankets and colored flags and balloons. When everyone had arrived, each with a secret smile, Peter announced, "All right, now is the time to say good-bye to you-know-who. Let's give him a good send-off. On your marks. Get set. Go!"

And all at once music and dancing, laughter and song exploded along the beach. Martin played a jig and danced at the same time. Jones the Farmer led Perkins and Snik in a chorus of "Roll Out the Barrel." Sophie the Dancer danced "Knees Up Mother Brown" at the edge of the waves. Mary stood on a sand dune and recited all the limericks she knew. And Peter just sat with a piece of kelp on his head and grinned.

The action continued until everyone got the giggles and had to lie down on the sand. After that they were all very hungry and they ate every scrap of fried chicken and barbecued fish, potato salad and coleslaw, cheese buns and chocolate cake and apple pie and ice cream. They drank all the lemonade and cider and iced tea. They ate every piece of watermelon and spit the seeds into the sea. And then just at dusk the sky cleared, so they scooped out comfy hollows and sand pillows along the shore and settled down to watch the sunset. It was a very purple sunset that night, and some folks thought it was really the Kibosh sinking into the sea. But other folks thought he had just hightailed it off over the hills. Whatever way he left, however, they all agreed he had gone for sure. And he didn't come back for a long, long time.

Sometimes it seems as if cheaters win, and the race goes to the swift after all. Vollstadt's story of a "good boy" may be reassuring in its simple message of obedience and kindness toward one's neighbors.

The Silver Dollar

By Elizabeth Weiss Vollstadt
Illustrated by Len Ebert

Silas Pinkham looked at the fine wool shawl in Mrs. Mitchell's shop window. It was deep blue and had thick, rich-looking tassels at each end.

"How Mama would love something as fancy as that!" he said to himself. Her old wrap was so thin and worn that by the end of last winter she had shivered whenever she went outside. If only he could buy her this one for her birthday next week!

Then he pushed the thought aside. There had been no extras in the Pinkham household for a long time. Papa had been away on a whaling voyage for almost four years now. Many other ships had returned to Nantucket this summer of 1841, weighted down with whale oil to light streets and homes all over the world. But Papa's ship was still far from home, and Mama had to be careful with the little money they had left.

Silas clutched the coins she had counted out for tea and turned into Mr. Turner's store. The delicious smells of chocolate, molasses, and spice made his stomach rumble. He stared at the maple sugar candy in a large wooden bin and wished he had an extra penny.

There was another customer already at the counter. From his weathered face and rough, faded clothes, Silas knew he was a sailor.

"Aye," the man was saying. "We passed right by the whaling ship *Ellen May*. And she was headed home for sure. Should be here before the week is out."

"Well, that'll be good news for plenty of folks around here," Mr. Turner said. "There's many a Nantucket man on her. Let's see, as I remember . . ."

He stopped when he saw Silas. "Hello there, young fellow. Are you going to try to get the silver dollar when the *Ellen May* arrives? I hear your cousin Reuben got one just last week."

Silas opened his brown eyes wide. Why hadn't he thought of that himself? Maybe he could buy Mama the fancy shawl after all! The captain's wife always gave a silver dollar to the first boy who brought news that her husband's ship was home. He was nine years old now and could outrun most boys his age. Surely he would have a chance.

A few minutes later, Mama's tea held tightly in his hand, Silas made his way through the crowded confusion of Straight Wharf at the end of Main Street. He was hoping to find out when the *Ellen May* would arrive at Nantucket.

But it was business as usual on the wharf. There was no undercurrent of excitement among the sailors as they unloaded incoming whalers or outfitted others for the long voyage halfway around the world.

"Hey, Silas! What're you doing here?"

Silas whirled around to face his cousin Reuben. "Just watchin'," he said. He wasn't going to tell Reuben about the *Ellen May*.

"I'm here on business," Reuben said proudly. "I just heard that the *Ellen May*

isn't too far from home, and I intend to earn me another silver dollar."

Silas's heart sank right down to his heavy, brown shoes. How could Reuben know already?

Sharp as always, Reuben noticed the disappointment on Silas's face. He grinned. "Hey, don't tell me you're here about the *Ellen May*, too!" He drew himself up tall to emphasize the three years' difference in their ages. "You might as well give up right now. You don't have a chance against me!"

"That's what you think," Silas retorted, trying to sound more confident than he felt. Somehow, he'd have to make sure he heard the news before Reuben.

The next morning, he raced through his chores so that he could get down to the harbor early. But as he dashed over the cobblestones of Main Street, *crash*! He ran headlong into Mrs. Mott, whose arms were filled with packages.

"Excuse me, ma'am," Silas mumbled apologetically. "I didn't mean . . . Here, I'll get these . . ."

Mrs. Mott's angry look softened as Silas hurried to pick up the packages that had scattered around. "Well, there's nothing that could break, so I guess there's no harm done. But why don't you help me bring these home, just in case I meet another young man in a hurry?"

Silas sighed. Another delay. Now he'd never make it to the wharf this morning. He had promised Mama he'd weed the vegetable garden before lunch.

Reluctantly, he shifted the packages to a more comfortable position and followed Mrs. Mott back up Main Street.

"Where were you heading in such a hurry?" she turned to ask.

"To the harbor. I want to ask about the *Ellen May*. I hear she's almost home, and I just have to be the first to bring the news to Mrs. Starbuck." Climbing the wooden steps

to Mrs. Mott's front porch, he told her about Mama's birthday and the fancy blue shawl.

Mrs. Mott smiled. "No wonder you were in such a hurry. I hope our little encounter didn't hurt your chances."

"Oh, I don't think so," Silas said politely. But as he trudged back home, he wasn't so sure. All he could do was hope that Reuben's day was as full of chores as his own.

It was late afternoon before he finally made it to the harbor. At first, he thought there would be no news again. Everying was quiet, the tall-masted ships deserted as most workers had stopped for their evening meal.

Then he noticed a small group of men clustered excitedly around two Nantucket sailors. As he drew nearer, he heard one of the sailors say, "It's the *Ellen May* comin' in, all right. We spotted her just a little while ago. Couldn't mistake that red and blue flag of hers."

Silas ran over to him. "Please sir, has anyone taken the news to Captain Starbuck's wife?"

The sailor smiled. "Not yet, lad. Go quickly and you'll get the silver dollar for sure."

Silas didn't waste any time. He turned and dashed toward Main Street, darting around whale oil casks and hopping over huge harpoon lines.

Suddenly, he saw his cousin Reuben saunter onto the wharf. *Oh no!* he thought. He ducked behind a large cask until Reuben was past. Now he'd really have to run fast. It was only a matter of seconds before Reuben heard the news, too.

Silas had just reached Main Street when he heard a whoop of delight behind him, followed by Reuben's footsteps pounding up the wharf and onto the cobblestones of Main Street. Silas ran as fast as he could, sprinting past Mrs. Mitchell's shop window with the

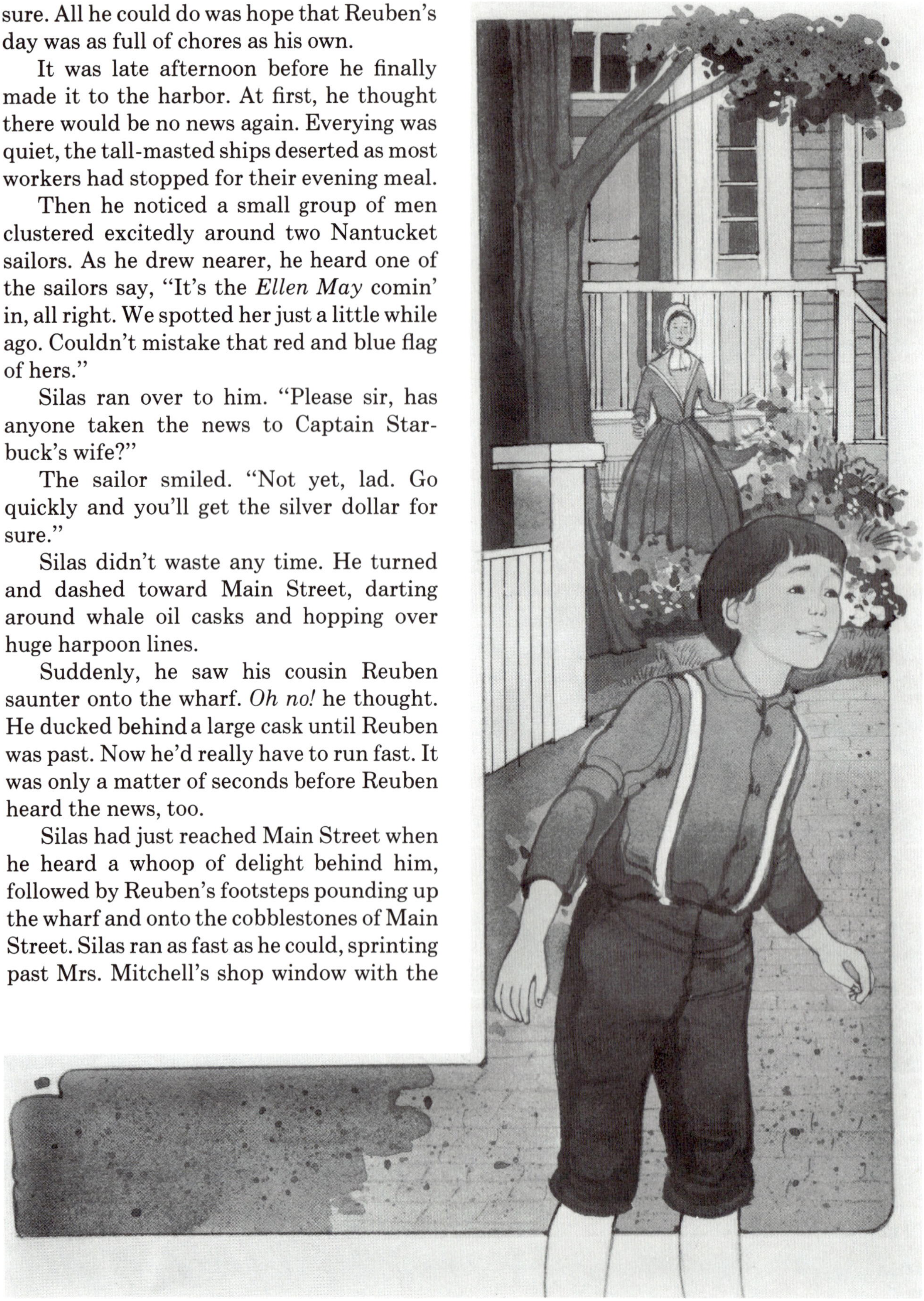

blue shawl in it, and jumping over a stool in front of Mr. Turner's store.

But he could still feel Reuben gaining. If only his legs were longer! Taking huge gulps of air, Silas pushed himself even harder. Now he was almost at Mrs. Mott's house, just a few doors down from Mrs. Starbuck's. He could see Mrs. Mott picking flowers in her front garden.

He was finally pulling away from Reuben when Mrs. Mott called, "Silas! Reuben! Boys! Come here!"

Her voice sounded so urgent, Silas couldn't help but slow down. That was just the advantage Reuben needed. He raced past Silas, laughing. He wasn't going to stop for Mrs. Mott, no matter what.

Fighting back tears, Silas watched Reuben turn into Captain Starbuck's front walk. The race for the silver dollar was over. He might as well see what Mrs. Mott wanted.

"How fortunate that I saw you," she said with a smile. "I was just picking some flowers for my guest, and I have enough for your mother. Come into the house and say hello while I sort these out."

Flowers! Silas thought. He had lost the silver dollar for some flowers! Glumly, he followed Mrs. Mott into her house. He didn't want to say hello to her guest. The only person he wanted to see was . . .

"Mrs. Starbuck!" The words tumbled out. He couldn't believe it. There was the captain's wife sitting in front of him, a cup of tea in her hand. His face lit up in a big grin.

"Mrs. Starbuck," he repeated. "The *Ellen May*! She's been sighted! Captain Starbuck should be in Nantucket by dawn tomorrow.

Mrs. Starbuck smiled at him. "What good news! I've been hearing rumors all day, but you're the first one to say they're really true. Thank you, Silas. And now, I have something for you."

She opened her purse and pulled out a shiny silver dollar. It was his.

A little later, Silas had the blue woolen shawl wrapped up in a fancy package. He also had just enough money left over to buy a small bag of maple sugar candy!

Consider the poor disrupted Florida communities and these homely interlopers; this article appeared in the September–October issue of International Wildlife.

Ugly Ducks Run Amok in Florida Towns

"Ugly ducklings" and "bilious creatures" are some of the nicer terms people use to describe the homely Muscovy ducks that are overrunning many Florida lawns and parks.

Native to South and Central America, the Muscovies were introduced to this country as an ornamental species in city parks. When they over-populated parks, they were released in other areas and quickly became a nuisance.

Though they do have their advocates, most people find Muscovies hard to love. With dull feathers and a blob of red wart-like skin covering their faces, they are less than beautiful. They hiss instead of quack, reproduce prolifically, and interbreed with native Florida duck species.

Gang warfare? Beak-stabbing? House raids? No, this is not your typical American neighborhood—this is a wild look at the natural behavior of a troublesome bunch of birds—and you may never think of Nature as a serene place again.

Starlings Are No Darlings

By Bill Lawren

Illustrated by Jeff Seaver

The nest box hangs unobtrusively about a third of the way up a light pole in a suburban parking lot. Rutgers University graduate student Phil Stouffer sneaks a ladder up underneath the box, lifts the lid and gently places an unhatched starling egg in the otherwise empty nest inside. The light blue egg is an "orphan," an intruder in the nest (the technical term is "parasite"), placed there as part of a manipulative experiment in starling behavior.

By surreptitiously putting the parasite egg in a nest where it does not belong. Stouffer and his advisor, sociobiologist Harry Power, hope to answer an important question about the behavior of starling "housewives." When the female bird returns to her nest, how will she respond to the presence of the parasite egg? Will she adopt it and hatch it as her own? Will she simply ignore it? Or will she do something that from a human point of view would seem to be almost unspeakably cruel?

Five minutes later the researchers have their answer. As they watch, the female starling returns and dives out of sight into the nest box. Then, she emerges seconds later carrying the egg in her beak. When she is a few feet away from the nest, she casually drops the egg from an altitude of about 15 feet. The rejected egg shatters on the pavement below.

In human society, this would be something akin to finding a baby on your doorstep, then dropping it from a ten-story window. But to Power, who has been studying starlings for more than a decade, it is simply one more aspect of the starling's behavioral repertoire—a repertoire that includes not only the sort of "ovicide" that he has just witnessed, but also house-stealing, gang terrorism, rampant promiscuity and even murder. In fact, says Power, when seen in all its conflict, drama and *sturm und drang*, starling society "makes Peyton Place look like a Sunday school."

Harry Power is a compact, square-jawed outdoorsman in his mid-forties. He looks like a young George C. Scott, but thinks and talks with the speed of a machine gun. His interest in bird behavior dates back to early childhood, when as a five-year-old he spent long afternoons running around his Los Angeles neighborhood with a salt shaker, trying to catch birds by salting their tails. Later, as a Montana high school student, he won a National Science Fair ecology award for pioneering work in the life history of mountain bluebirds—work which he continued to pursue as a postdoctoral student.

But simply observing and cataloging bird behavior was not enough for Power. He wanted to know how that behavior evolved, how it helped the creatures survive and whether or not there were general principles underlying that behavior that might be applied to other species, even people. To get at those bigger questions, he needed large populations of essentially tractable birds as subjects for what he calls "crash-bang experiments"—experiments in which the seamy side of bird behavior can be revealed by, he says, "getting the animal to do something you wouldn't otherwise see."

Power found bluebirds less than suitable for this kind of experiment. But in starlings—a European bird introduced to the United States in the 1890s which has since spread to 49 states, northern Mexico and southern Canada—he found the innate "nastiness" he was seeking. He also found the naturally dense populations and the durability that made for more complex experiments—and, perhaps, closer analogies with human society. "Starlings are much more like us than bluebirds are," he says. "In fact, when we look at them, to some extent we're looking at a morality play of ourselves.

To better understand this morality play, Power began in 1978 to construct what amounted to his own personal starling colony on the Rutgers campus. Over the next ten years, he and his students augmented an existing colony by building more than 125 new nest boxes and hanging them on light stanchions and telephone poles all over the suburban New Jersey campus. As the starlings took up residence and built nests in the man-made boxes, the scientists kept careful track of the birds by marking and banding them, and even by dyeing each embryo a different color just before it hatched so that they could tell exactly which egg produced each hatchling.

To make a precise determination of which parents had sired which offspring, the researchers did hundreds of detailed biopsies, including sophisticated genetic tests to help establish family lines. And they augmented all this by keeping the nest boxes under steady observation. Over the years these exhaustive procedures enabled Power and his students to compile a virtual encyclopedia of data, information which has allowed them to paint the most detailed picture available of life among the starlings.

And as it turns out, it is a very difficult life.

Among starlings, as in many other birds, the nest is the cornerstone of society—home, nursery and status symbol rolled into one. Just prior to breeding season in the spring, competition among male starlings for nesting sites reaches proportions more intense than anything seen among humans, even in the great American land rushes of the nineteenth century.

"The male birds get in knock-down, drag-out fights," says Power. "They'll get down on the ground and stand on one another and just *pound*." The winners of these battles gain not only the nesting site, but the right to crow about their victory to the females.

Like people, starlings appear to have a discriminating eye not only for the best homes, but also for the best neighborhoods. On a tour of his far-flung colony, Power points out a string of some seven light poles with nest boxes that comprise a sort of starling Beverly Hills. "Those boxes always attract the oldest and the most productive birds," he says. "In fact, they'll kill to retain those boxes."

The reason for the desirability of this "neighborhood," however, remains a mystery. "What's so great about those particular boxes?" asks Power. "It could be that they're close to the best food supply, or it could be something social that's not apparent to us. We just don't know."

While the most successful birds establish their claims to Beverly Hills and others settle for different boxes, the least successful starlings simply run out of acceptable nesting sites. They are left to wander the area as homeless "floaters." But floaters are no less interested in reproducing than their more successful counterparts. Consequently, Power learned, these outcast nestless birds resort to a number of wily strategies to provide home and hatching for their offspring.

In the absence of a nest of their own, for example, female floaters often will try to slip their own eggs into another bird's nest. Such egg parasitism rests on a curious perceptual disability that characterizes not only starlings but most birds: females frequently cannot tell their own eggs from those of another bird of the same species. (Only when the nest is empty and an egg suddenly appears, as in the manipulated experiment that began this article, does the female recognize it as that of a stranger and discard it.)

Once a female has laid her own eggs, she can be victimized easily by a floater that sneaks into the nest when the resident female is out and adds an egg of her own to the clutch. The unknowing resident then hatches the egg and raises the chick as if it were her own. By marking eggs in nests and watching for the appearance of unmarked floater eggs, Power has found that this parasitism occurs with astonishing frequency: one in three starling nests contains at least one parasite egg.

Since it is obviously not in the resident female's interest to expend energy and resources in raising someone else's young, how does she defend against being victimized by floaters and their parasite eggs? Power has a theory: resident females defend against parasitism, he thinks, by taking out a sort of insurance against it. "Our studies," he explains, "show that the most productive clutch size—the size that produces the most surviving chicks—is six. But the most *common* clutch size is five. Why the discrepancy? Well, if you start with six eggs and then a parasite egg comes along, the clutch size goes to seven, and at that size the number of surviving chicks falls way off. But if you only have five eggs and are parasitized to six—you achieve the size that produces the most survivors. I think that birds are in effect leaving space for parasite eggs, not because they want them, but because they want to make sure they don't get pushed off the productivity cusp."

Although egg parasitism may provide floaters with at least some opportunity to perpetuate their genes, most of these birds would be much more successful if they had nest sites of their own. As a result, many homeless starlings will try to actually steal an already established nest. The technique is simple. "The floater bird invades the established nest, throws all the eggs out and just takes it over," says Power.

Attempts at this dual crime—house-stealing and mass "ovicide"—occur in about 12 percent of all the nest boxes under Power's observation, and are sometimes the work not of lone birds but of gangs of up to 13 members. In fact, in one particular group of nest boxes at Rutgers, a sort of gang warfare has been rampant for years. "But the success of these gangs," notes Power, "is very low. They'll come in, lay a few eggs and then some other starling pushes *them* out."

Obviously, the ongoing struggle for real estate is the source of a tremendous amount of conflict in starling society. But the same is true, Power has found, of sexual politics. He illustrates his point by showing a visitor a rich lawn where hundreds of starlings are feeding.

"When you look at the birds carefully," he says, "you realize that they're feeding in male-female pairs, with the male and female not more than a foot apart. In these pairs it's always the female who leads and the male who follows. What the male is doing is literally protecting her rear—and, of course, his genes. If the female gets too far away, or if the male gets distracted, other males will display at her, lunge and attempt to mount her. So the male wants to make sure that she doesn't pick up any sperm but his."

Starlings rarely stay with a mate longer than one season, and the females are not the only ones with roving eyes. "Once the couple gets back to the nest, and the male is sure the female is secure, he might fly over to the next nest box and try to mount his neighbor's wife," says Power. The scientist believes that the female's coquettish availability to other males is an evolutionary strategy designed to keep the male so busy guarding her he has little time for sexual adventuring of his own.

These stratagems do seem to keep rates of successful cuckoldry surprisingly low. By conducting genetic studies of parents and their chicks in 95 nests, Power determined that only 2 to 8 percent of the offspring were illegitimate. *Attempts* apparently are legion. "If we had the same frequency of cuckoldry attempts in our society," he says, "you couldn't trust your wife or husband to go to the market."

Needless to say, however, cuckoldry is relatively inoffensive compared to another common aspect of starling behavior: the killing of their own kind. In winter, for example, starlings will kill for the chance to roost in a nest box, locking their legs around one another and stabbing at each other's faces until one of the combatants is dead. In fact, one female starling under Power's observation seemed to have an ongoing propensity for this kind of violence. "Sometimes when we came up to do a nest box census," he recalls, "there she'd be, locked in mortal combat with yet another bird. We must have 'saved' her four times in two years."

Because starlings disperse as far as 50 miles after they leave the nest, it is virtually impossible to tell how many of them eventually are killed. But the bodies of dead starlings with telltale beak marks on their faces turn up often enough that Power infers a murder rate among starlings of as much as 10 percent.

Power is quick to note that none of this seemingly violent behavior is unique to starlings. Wood ducks often practice parasitism, for instance, while cuckoldry is common among bobolinks and egg removal occurs frequently among cliff swallows. What's more, there are reports of lethal fighting in a variety of bird species.

For all its turmoil and strife, starling society has its gentler and more cooperative side. Power notes, for example, that starlings are "very good parents. They're not easily frightened away from their young, and they take good care of them."

In the end, then, Power tries to avoid making sweeping value judgments. "Nature," he says, "is neither moral nor immoral. To have a realistic view, you have to have an amoral view."

Some critics have argued that Power's "crash-bang" experiments might produce starling behavior that is something other than the "natural" acts that occur in the wild. But, says the scientist, "we're not changing the birds' behavior by giving them things like drugs. We haven't even increased their natural population densities, so the behavior we see is not the result of overcrowding. These birds are doing exactly as they please. Whether or not it's 'natural' is one thing. But it sure as heck is wild!"

What's your idea of paradise? Unlimited television, no school, and cheeseburgers at every meal? A room full of books and no afterschool chores? Almost everyone has an idea of the perfect place to live and work. Naomi Segal looks at the idealized places people have created in the pursuit of maximum happiness.

Building Heaven on Earth: America's Utopian Communities

By Naomi Segal

Why would a person leave mainstream society and venture out to form a new one? In 1824, more than 1,000 men and women responded to signs inviting all "industrious and well-disposed" people to join a new community in New Harmony, Indiana. The community's founder, a wealthy Englishman named Robert Owen, promised them an "empire of peace and goodwill." The offer sounded good, but what did it mean?

Owen believed that the Industrial Revolution had caused many of society's problems. As superintendent of a cotton mill in the village of New Lanark, Scotland, Owen had turned a run-down village into a model community by increasing wages, shortening the workday, and building new houses. He believed that all of society should be divided into communities of 500 to 2,000 people, with each community providing members with clothing, shelter, and good working conditions. In each community, Owen envisioned, a complex of buildings where people would live and eat would be set up in a square around a green. Gardens and playgrounds would be inside and outside the green. Members would work in agriculture and manufacturing. Although New Harmony never progressed beyond some log cabins, it was a first step toward a new society.

At New Harmony, things went well at first. People attended lectures, danced in the Hall of New Harmony, and read. Owen decided to declare this trial settlement a success. But conflicts began to break out among members—sometimes over little things, such as what clothes men would wear, or larger things, such as unequal efforts at work. Some people had come to New Harmony expecting to find a paradise, not to help build one. New Harmony's financial debt grew because no one would work. In 1828, New Harmony closed.

Communal Living in America

New Harmony failed, but it was only the beginning of a long list of attempts to establish utopian communities in the United States. *Utopia*, a word that means *no place*, is also the title of a book by Saint Thomas More, published in 1516. It tells about the travels of a sailor to an island called Utopia, where all people are equal, prosperous, educated, and wise. During the 1800s, many communities based on their founders' vision of an ideal society were formed. Many of them were based on the idea of communal (group) living: sharing property, work, and income. The idea itself was not new to the U.S. religious groups that had fled from persecution in Europe during the 1800s and earlier found that, by pooling their resources, they had a better chance for survival. Most of the groups created in the latter half of the 19th century were secular (nonreligious).

"We are all a little wild here with numberless projects of social reform," wrote the philosopher Ralph Waldo Emerson to a friend in 1840. "Not a reading man but has a draft of a new community in his waistcoat pocket."

Every Day a Picnic

Some communities started out as social experiments, rather than as examples for society to come. In 1841, a young minister named George Ripley founded Brook Farm in West Roxbury, Massachussetts. Ripley wanted to create a liberal (unrestricted) community of intellectuals. Money to purchase the farmland and buildings was raised by requiring members to purchase shares in the farm. Additional money would come from vegetable sales and tuition from the Brook Farm School.

Life on Brook Farm must have seemed strange to the people who lived nearby. Imagine, a dairy farm run by people who did not know the first thing about cows, or how to tend a garden! The school had no specific study hours and held classes just about everywhere: alongside the brook, in the kitchen, in the chicken house. Strangest of all, the people at Brook Farm shared everything—farm chores, income, and property.

Yet students flocked to the school, and intellectuals such as Ralph Waldo Emerson and Nathaniel Hawthorne visited often. For Brook Farmers, harmony between work and the mind was part of their vision of an ideal society.

Georgiana Bruce, a young British governess who worked in Brook Farm's infant school, found life there ideal indeed: "What a royal time we had," she wrote. "The days were full of affection and sunshine . . . . The air seemed to hold more exhilarating qualities than any I had breathed before. . . . Had the world denied you opportunity for education? Here your highest needs should be satisfied. . . . What a heavenly world this is getting to be!"

Can't Live on Harmony

That harmony was not enough to support the farm, however. As Brook Farm entered its third year with a steady deficit (debt), the members decided to reorganize. In 1844, Brook Farm became a phalanx (*FAYlanks*) based on the philosophy of Charles Fourier, a French philosopher. (A *phalanx* is an organized body of persons.) Fourier believed that communes should be set up with 1,600–1,800 people, who would live and work together, but could also have some personal property.

With the reorganization, new members joined Brook Farm, causing a rift between the old members and the new. The day after being completed, the community's main building burned down. Brook Farm dissolved in 1846.

Heaven on Earth

Why did many secular utopian communities—Brook Farm, for example—fail? One reason was that they had no unity.

"They quarrel about their religion. They quarrel about their food. They dispute about carrying out their principles," wrote John Humphrey Noyes, founder of the Oneida (*oh-NYE-duh*) Community.

Oneida was probably the most successful of all the utopian communities. It began in Putney, Vermont, but so upset local residents that Noyes had to flee to escape lynching. Noyes had set up a socialist system in which people shared all personal possessions and lived as one family.

Noyes moved his community to Oneida, New York, where it flourished. Income came from farming, manufacturing, and the making of silverware. But in 1880, the members of the community turned Oneida into a joint-stock company. Capitalism triumphed over socialism.

The Shakers

One of the most well-known utopian groups was the Shakers, whose name comes from its members' religious dancing. In 1774, Ann Lee, a Shaker, arrived in the U.S. with some followers. The first communal village of Shakers was established in New Lebanon, New York, in 1787. By 1835, there were over 5,000 Shakers living in 18 settlements.

The Shaker life-style required a closely knit, almost closed-off community. The Shakers lived a strict and simple life. In their devotion to God, they prohibited (banned) relationships between men and women. The Shakers had no children of their own, but adopted orphans.

Shaker life was devoted to work. In the summer they awoke at 4:30 a.m., in the winter at 5 a.m. They produced highly crafted furniture, tools, and other goods that the "outside" world valued.

At night, the Shakers would hang their chairs on pegs that lined the walls, and step out onto a well-oiled dance floor. Although some people consider the Shaker life-style grim, most Shakers themselves were happy. They did not force anyone to stay. But, by 1875, their numbers had dwindled. Many young people left after learning a trade and few new members took their place.

By the 1880s, utopian settlements in the U.S. had dwindled in number. Secular movements disbanded when members could not get along. Many of the religious groups dwindled because fewer members joined them or because they had slowly eroded their ways to follow a more worldly life-style. However, both secular and religious communities had left many values behind—equality between men and women, for example, and liberal education. Many religious groups, such as the Shakers, also left us tools as well as beautiful furniture, quilts, and other crafted goods in which they had specialized to support themselves.

The Farm at Twin Oaks

Communes have not disappeared in America. Today, there are as many as 1,000 such groups in the U.S.

Ben, 12, grew up at Springtree Farm, a small commune in rural Virginia.

"It's like living in a large family, except not everyone is related," he says. "Sometimes I feel like I don't have enough privacy. But I also have more things to do than other kids."

Ben likes to explore the woods and river nearby. And he helps tend the animals and garden that provide most of the commune's food. Springtree is a small community, with only eight adults. But other such groups, such as Twin Oaks, also in Virginia, have more than 70.

Springtree members share all income. Twin Oaks is supported by a successful hammock-making business. Although people in communes follow a different life-style, they also interact with regular society by attending local schools, shopping, and using the local library and other community facilities.

"All of our kids are out now," says Toots, an 11-year Springtree member. "We just hope they take the positive values they learned here and reinforce them in their own lives."

Perhaps good neighbors—perfect neighbors—would share a garden similar to this one, which is permanently framed by a window of the Adachi Museum in western Honshu, Japan. The photograph was first published in an article about Japanese gardens in National Geographic.

Framed Garden

Photograph by Michael S. Yamashita

A fence divides the gardens of these two souls—one cranky, the other friendly. But as you'll see in this story, the ways of nature bow to no boundaries. If good fences make good neighbors, then bad fences make good pumpkins.

Mr. Runkle's Pumpkin

By Betse Brydon

Mr. Runkle stroked his trim beard, speckled brown and white like the breast of a sparrow. "Neat and tidy, neat and tidy," he murmured, looking out at his garden. Not a weed in sight. Not a bug hiding anywhere. The corn marched in orderly rows; the beans, straight as the jars of food lining his pantry shelves (in alphabetical order). And the pumpkins! Training the wandering green vines had been a difficult task, but now they grew in a beeline toward the fence.

"Neat and tidy," he said again, picking up his copy of the Stonylake Annual Fair book. He opened it to the vegetable section and began marking his entries. But he couldn't concentrate on filling out the form. Something nagged at the back of his mind. Something about the fence.

Mr. Runkle frowned and looked at the fence that separated his garden from the one next-door. Some sort of yellow, weedy thing nodded its ragged head at him from the other side. The lemony spot marred the evenness of fence and sky. Mr. Runkle reached past the can of bug spray for the pruning shears. Standing on a handy crate, he prepared to snip the bold bloom.

"Don't you dare!" On the other side of the fence stood a tiny woman with sparkling eyes. Bits of leaves clung to her wispy, mouse-colored hair escaping from under her battered straw hat. She shook her garden trowel at Mr. Runkle. Lumps of mud flew about wildly.

"You leave my pretty flowers alone, do you hear?" She tried to look stern, but failed with a smile.

Mr. Runkle sniffed. "Miss Appleby, your garden is a mess. There is no order to it, no order at all. There are weeds and bugs everywhere. It is a disgrace!"

Miss Appleby wiped her hands on her apron, bright with blue and green roses. She looked around her garden, as though seeing it for the first time.

"These 'weeds,' as you call them, are beautiful flowers. The 'bugs' are dancing butterflies and bees gathering pollen. In the evenings I can sit on my porch and watch the fireflies light up. I can hear the crickets chirp and smell the perfume from those 'weeds.' Weeds indeed!"

Mr. Runkle sniffed and rolled his eyes. "Please try and keep YOUR garden on YOUR side of the fence, Miss Appleby."

He turned sharply and paraded away. Miss Appleby sighed and shook her head.

As Mr. Runkle entered his small, spotless house with relief, he thought with a shudder of the hopeless disarray in the cottage next-door. Books with leaves sticking out, old newspapers stuffed in couch cushions, a brown apple core in a stained teacup —and dust everywhere. He had only been in Miss Appleby's house once, but he would never forget it.

"Disgraceful. Inside and out," he said aloud and whisked away a few specks of dust. Then he carefully locked the door behind him and marched down the sidewalk toward town.

As he passed Miss Appleby's house, he quickly glanced into her garden.

"I wonder what new weeds are growing there today." Mr. Runkle peered through the shrubbery. With a surprised snort, he halted in midstep, his eyes bulging.

Birds sang in the trees. Butterflies hovered over a jungle of rainbow-colored flowers. Insects buzzed and hummed. The sweet scent and the bright colors reminded Mr. Runkle of the sugary cereal section in the grocery store. But what stopped him so abruptly was the sight of a huge pumpkin. An ENORMOUS pumpkin.

"What . . . How . . . ," he sputtered. "How did she do it?" He thought of the small, unimportant pumpkin growing neatly in his own garden.

"I don't understand it. My pumpkin should be much bigger." He went on to town where he filled a shopping bag at the Stonylake Garden Center with spray cans and boxes.

The next day Mr. Runkle carefully poured fertilizer over the pumpkin's roots. He sprayed it with Bugnot. He pulled all the tiny weeds. He straightened a few stray leaves. Day after day he tended his pumpkin. On the other side of the fence, Miss Appleby's pumpkin thrived on what seemed to be neglect. It smothered weeds and flowers alike. It provided shade for chipmunks and a seat for Miss Appleby. It grew and grew until it was bigger than a beach ball, bigger than a TV set. Mr. Runkle stopped looking. His pumpkin, like an orange- and green-streaked volleyball, lost a few leaves.

The day of the Stonylake Annual Fair arrived at last. Mr. Runkle gathered his straightest carrots, his roundest red tomatoes, and the most perfect of his other well-trained vegetables. He packed them carefully in shiny wire baskets and walked sadly to the fairgrounds, leaving his pumpkin behind.

Flags fluttered in the breeze; children laughed and shrieked. Mr. Runkle trudged through the dust. The smell of popcorn and caged animals filled the air. After leaving his vegetables at the judging tent, Mr. Runkle strolled around stiffly, looking at the exhibits. Between a display of lawn tractors and a booth selling hot dogs on a stick, he caught sight of Miss Appleby struggling up the hill to the judging tent. She was pushing her gigantic pumpkin in a wheelbarrow, her face red as a beet.

Mr. Runkle sniffed and looked the other way. Why should I help her, he thought, She's going to win anyway.

The next day Mr. Runkle hurried to the fairgrounds. Passing Miss Appleby's gate, he saw her locking her door. Mr. Runkle walked faster. Miss Appleby overtook him at the corner.

"Going to the fair?" she asked, smiling sweetly at him. "Mind if I walk with you?"

"If you like," he answered, walking so briskly that Miss Appleby had to trot to keep up.

"I'm sure all your nice vegetables won prizes," she said, panting a little.

Mr. Runkle sniffed.

As they entered the vegetable tent, Miss Appleby took his arm, preventing him from making a polite escape.

"Look!" she exclaimed in front of the carrot table. "You have a red ribbon on your carrots."

"Second prize." He scowled. "They weren't straight enough."

His tomatoes and corn wore blue ribbons. First prize, Mr. Runkle sniffed smugly. The pumpkins, piled high on a table, were next. The largest pumpkin, Miss Appleby's, was adorned with a blue ribbon. Beside it stood a silver trophy for Best-of-Show.

"Congratulations, Miss Appleby," Mr. Runkle said curtly. He started to move to the next exhibit.

"Wait." Miss Appleby grabbed Mr. Runkle's arm. "Look at the pumpkin."

Mr. Runkle glanced at it again, rolling his eyes. Then he stared at it, almost choking on a disdainful sniff. He turned to Miss Appleby, his mouth opening and shutting like a fish.

"I don't understand," he said finally. "It has my name on it."

"It's your pumpkin," said Miss Appleby. "The vine escaped through a crack in the fence. I just left it alone. You did all the work."

"But I was so rude to you. Why didn't you just cut the vine off?"

"I like to let nature take its own course. And look how it turned out," she said, pointing to the prizewinning pumpkin.

On the walk home, Mr. Runkle stopped in the Stonylake Garden Center and bought a book on flowers.

"I was thinking of putting in a few marigolds," he explained to Miss Appleby with a small sniff, "just to keep the vegetables company."

Highlights has had some of the best covers this year, always asking readers to find the deliberate mistakes in the illustration. But what's really wrong with a community of elves wearing tea cups for hats, or tending books growing on trees? Somehow, in this miniature neighborhood, it doesn't look wrong—just fun.

Busy Elves

Illustration by John O'Brien

Home is home, and in the barrios of East Harlem you'll find young men such as Tany Davila, who has 175 hand-groomed pigeons that soar over the tenements. Jere Van Dyk explores the lighted places of a poor urban neighborhood.

Growing Up in East Harlem

By Jere Van Dyk

It was calm and hot as I watched the barrio waking up for another Saturday. A man worked under a car, the wash flapped on a rooftop line, Latin music throbbed up from the street. Someone made strong coffee and new bread.

From the roof of a high rise that was littered with crack cocaine vials and broken bottles, I could see the green fields of Central Park, a sailboat tacking on the East River, the glittering skyscrapers of midtown Manhattan, a world away.

In the middle was East Harlem itself: brownstone tenements, housing projects, vacant lots, burned-out buildings, shattered windows—200 square blocks where 120,000 people live beset by drugs, crime, and despair but also in a cousinship of hope, love, and optimism that stirs the outsider.

Fifty percent of the people are of Hispanic origin, 49 percent black, a few others of Italian or Asian ancestry. Per capita income hovers around $4,000. One in seven East Harlem adults is out of work. More than one in three gets some form of public assistance, among the highest welfare rates in the nation. The area has some of the city's worst crime and one of the nation's highest school-dropout rates. Drugs and AIDS haunt every man, woman, and child who lives here.

To live in Spanish Harlem—the neighborhood, *el barrio*—you must watch yourself and everyone else, because you are in another world; you are, as my friend Joe Rodriguez told me on my first day, "across the line."

"Don't stare. Be cool," Joe said. He had been here, he spoke the language. "It's all body language," Joe said, showing me how. "Look up and ahead, never down. Do a beeline. Keep your hands out of your pockets."

Walking along Third Avenue, we passed a stand selling yucca, yams, *batata*, *plátanos*, mangoes. Then we came to a bad corner, Lexington and 110th Street, filled with people with quick eyes and dark clothes.

"Three star, three star," a man shouted, hawking cocaine. "Methadone 60, 80," said another, advertising synthetic heroin. A man with his hair in dreadlocks silently held out two hypodermic needles in a wrapper.

No so long ago, it was different.

"This was a nice community," recalls Pete Pascale, 75, remembering the simple East Harlem of his youth. The neighborhood was known then as Little Italy, a place of two-cent ice creams, ten-cent movies, unlocked doors, kerosene lamps, and a policeman on the corner who knew your name and your reputation.

"People worked hard," Pascale says, his face reflecting the pleasant memory. "There was respect for the family."

Even today you catch glimpses of what it must have been like—in community vegetable gardens that thrive in vacant lots, in a school classroom where kids talk about the future, in the hospital where a doctor hugs two children she has known since they were born, in a church parade on a summer night.

I watched the 105th annual procession of Our Lady of Mount Carmel coming up 116th Street. The faithful—Hispanics, blacks, and whites—walked together at a solemn pace, candles flickering in the dark, following a plaster Madonna on a float, led by a brass band whose members wore black pants and red berets. These were proud people any American would recognize, people who cared about their neighborhood. Seeing them made me realize that there are pockets of calm just beneath the barrio's turbulent surface.

BRUCE DAVIDSON/MAGNUM

A little girl and a bird in its cage look out their windows on East 100th Street in East Harlem.

Lugo's Barbershop on Lexington Avenue is a warm place where neighbors can talk, surrounded by color maps of San Juan and Puerto Rico. Relaxed families smile from snapshots on display. Inspirational, handwritten mottoes are posted on the walls: "Never become a victim of fear or envy; that will keep you from doing good." "He who has obstacles and overcomes them is the winner."

The man behind the mottoes, Alejandro Lugo, ran a comb through his customer's hair. "You find good and bad all over the world," he said. "I always wanted to come to this country. I saw the big buildings in a dream when I was a boy living in Mayagüez." Since 1952 Alejandro has lived in the barrio, and he intends to stay.

Alejandro is a Puerto Rican, belonging to the next-to-last wave of immigrants in the barrio. The first Europeans to arrive were the Dutch, who came in the mid-1600s. They imported African slaves. Two Dutch brothers, Hendrick and Isaac DeForest, were among the earliest settlers, breaking land for a small farm by the river. A village called New Haarlem, named for the city in Holland, flourished there. The English came

KATRINA THOMAS/PHOTO RESEARCHERS

A young boy at night looks at the bright lights of the Triborough Bridge from 104th Street in East Harlem.

next, then the Germans, Irish, and Swiss. Each group prospered in turn and was joined by the next wave of immigrants speaking a new language but looking for the old opportunities, working for low wages in sweatshops.

Jews and Italians came in the 1890s, fleeing Manhattan's overcrowded Lower East Side. The new immigrants worked in the needle trade, sewing garments. When those workers moved on, the garment industry recruited new ones from Puerto Rico. By 1930 some 45,000 Puerto Ricans lived in East Harlem. They still predominate there, though newcomers arrive steadily from poor Caribbean countries and from war-ravaged Central America.

"I was an orphan," said Alejandro. He put his scissors down. "A nun took me in and sent me to Catholic school. Now I try to give back. I am a deacon of the street." On Sundays Alejandro closes his shop and changes into a long robe for services at St. Cecilia's, the cathedral of the barrio, as it is called. During the week he visits the sick, teaches the Bible to children, and lends an ear to neighbors in trouble.

I watched him speak to the congregation at St. Cecilia's. "We see miracles every day," he said fervently. "Herod wanted to kill the children, and no one helped prevent it. Today we can care for our children."

You want to believe his words when you look around the church. There were altar boys with jeans and running shoes showing beneath their robes, altar girls in dark dresses, and uncertain new immigrants with their hair wetted down. The building was packed, and the worshipers clapped as they sang. Father Norman Simmons delivered the homily in Spanish, and when the Mass was finished, chidren ran up and down the aisles.

Outside St. Cecilia's, after the service, the sun was bright and the air smelled fresh after a hard rain, and on the church corner two disposable hypodermic needles glistened in a puddle. Under streetlights, people stood around, leaned on double-parked cars, sat on stoops. Three motorcycles shot by, screaming in the night.

Every morning for weeks I went into the barrio, and every evening I walked slowly out again, past where it abruptly ends at 96th Street. Walking down Park Avenue, I felt the eyes of uniformed doormen of elegant granite buildings examining my unshaven face, my old jeans and running shoes. It didn't matter if they thought I was from the barrio; I knew I was only a visitor there. You had to be born in the barrio to understand it, to know what really made it tick. Fear, crime, violence, drugs—that was the frightening exterior you read about and saw.

It was the humanity that drew you in: The ice-cream man with the drooping mustache tending his wooden cart, Mexican-American boys selling flowers on the corner, weekend baseball on a neat diamond near the river, a happy man crossing the street to shake a friend's hand, kids practicing rap music on the corner, dressy little girls playing hopscotch in the park.

There were people like Dr. Nabil Saad and Raymond Cornbill, who help run North General Hospital, a small 200-bed facility on 124th Street.

"We take everyone who walks in the door," said Nabil Saad, Egyptian-born president of the medical staff and chief of pediatrics. "We accept the poorest of the poor."

"Even if they can't pay," said Raymond Cornbill, chief operating officer, "we have a moral obligation."

It's clear that things here are tough. Life is on the edge—big families, small incomes. The hospital's staff does indeed see some of the most desperate cases in the barrio—the homeless people with venereal disease, the tuberculosis patients, the AIDS victims. But East Harlem isn't all drugs and crime.

I came to know many of those residents—people who work, send their kids to school, shop in the little stores that open for business every day. Self-reliance, usefulness, responsibility—that is their code.

"I've worked for everything I've got," said Maria Penton, showing me her airy loft on 107th Street. Around us were rows of sewing machines, ironing boards, a time clock, dresses on metal racks—the tools of her successful dressmaking business.

"Too many people lost their self-esteem when they came from Puerto Rico," she said. "The government gave them apartments, clothing, furniture; it made the people shrivel up and die." Maria has lived in the barrio since 1948. She has witnessed gang wars, crack fights, decay.

She pointed a finger at me. "They created a monster! All those generations of welfare! There is no respect any more because people haven't worked."

But she is proud of her accomplishments. She showed me some black cotton dresses with puffed sleeves. "I can give you this dress in ten days. Hong Kong takes longer. That's how I can make it."

Children play an animated game of dominoes, a favorite pastime of both children and adults in East Harlem. Grocery stores (or bodegas) often serve as gathering places in Latin communities.

© MARTHA COOPER/CITY LORE

She starts her workers at minimum wage and gives them four raises a year. She pointed to a man lugging dresses around—her husband.

"I offered him what he was making at his other job," she said. "He accepted." She lit another cigarette. "I'm the boss here. He's the boss at home."

Third Avenue, like 116th Street, is a business district, where sidewalks are filled with racks of shirts and dresses. Store owners are often Asian. Corner groceries are run by families from the Dominican Republic. Yemenite Arabs operate the candy stores, bought from Jews. Koreans run vegetable stands and fish stores. Chinese are buying whole buildings.

Near 118th Street, I saw a sign in a window full of televisions, lamps, furniture: "Muebleria Kosches, Est. 1888." Inside, Robert Kosches finished talking in Spanish to a young couple and walked me to the back of his store.

Robert had grown up in the neighborhood but now commuted from New Jersey. "My grandfather, who came from Austria, started this business," he said, switching to English.

He is hopeful. "There is a tremendous market up there. I get calls from real estate agents every day," he said, pointing across the street to Inner City Sports, Casa Elegante, McDonald's, all newcomers. Several streets away a mosque for New York's thriving Islamic community is rising.

Since 1988, when East Harlem was designated as a state economic-development zone, land appraisals have climbed. Businesses can qualify for utility subsidies, generous construction loans, and tax breaks, based on the size of their investment and the number of local people they employ. Urban homesteaders, who renovate old tenements and buy them from the city at bargain rates, are beginning to change the face of the neighborhood as well.

Walking up Second Avenue, I came across a young man with a carpenter's tool belt slung over his shoulder. His boss, David Calvert, of Youth Action Homes, explained what the carpenter was doing.

"We take old buildings that have been foreclosed by the city and rehabilitate them for homeless people," David said. Kids from East Harlem, where the program originated more than a decade ago, do the work.

Ramon Nuñez, the carpenter I had seen in the street, put down his tools and looked me in the eye. "I feel more responsible now. I'd rather work, take my time, do it right."

Ramon, one of 36 youths under David Calvert's instruction, works a week, goes to school a week. If Ramon stays off drugs and sticks with it for a year, he will receive a high school diploma, a driver's license, and a permanent job. Most trainees make good, with 40 to 60 youths advancing to full-time jobs each year—at 20 percent over the minimum wage.

Their work was good. In the newly renovated apartment the molding hugged the corners, the bathroom door hung straight, the closet doors shut tightly.

What about life on the streets?

A tall, thin boy spoke up. "I envy the drug dealers sometimes, but it's not worth it," he said, referring to the gold chains and the $80 running shoes that pitchers and runners and carriers can buy with the profits of their trade. His jeans and work boots were covered with dust from work. He was an appealing young man, 17 years old, polite, soft-spoken. He had a nice smile. I'll call him Roberto.

What about the future?

"This is New York City," said Roberto. "You never know what might happen."

A few weeks later I heard that Roberto had been shot in a street dispute over drugs.

School children in East Harlem watch the Three Kings Parade which celebrates, on January 6th, the Epiphany or the arrival of the three wise men in Bethlehem. The parade is an adaptation of a Puerto Rican tradition in which men from the community dress up as the three kings and visit children in the neighborhoods.

He would survive, but life would be different now that he was out of David Calvert's program.

"People are struggling against great odds," said Sister Judy Garson, leading me into a brownstone town house with bars on the windows and a steel gate on the door. The Little Sisters of the Assumption and other volunteers work out of this house, helping barrio families with food, nursing care, child care, advice. The Little Sisters have been here for 30 years.

"Believing in yourself is so important," said Sister Judy, as another nun put aside groceries for a young mother. "Often the only time a woman is praised is when she produces a beautiful baby. It's two steps forward, one back. But people *are* making it."

Luz Maldonado, 32, is one of them. "My husband left me, but I've got my feet on the ground," said Luz, a gregarious woman who drops by the Little Sisters' house regularly. She sat with her baby, Marisa, who seemed healthy and well cared for.

"Coming here, being with the Little Sisters, I know I'm not alone," Luz said, upbeat, smiling again. "I'm going to college at night." She took off her coat, put it aside, and looked lovingly at her daughter. "I'm going to make it," she said.

Women like Luz keep the barrio glued together. The percentage of households in East Harlem headed by women—48 percent—is among the highest in the U. S. While men play dominoes in the shade or drink from brown paper bags on the corner, women take care of the family. I saw them day after day, walking the kids to school in clean clothes they can be proud of, waiting for them in the afternoons, making sure they got past the dealers. Women often make the difference between a child who survives and one who dies early.

I met youths who study hard and look to the future at the Manhattan Center for Science and Mathematics, a consolidated grade school, junior high, and high school on 116th Street. Once known as the Drug Store, for the illicit business openly conducted there, the school now attracts national attention for academic excellence. The student body is 98 percent black and Hispanic. The school's dropout rate is less than 2 percent, well below the city average of 40 percent. Some 90 percent of its students rank at or above their grade levels in reading tests, and nearly 100 percent of its graduates go on to college.

"When I came here four years ago, there was no running water in the bathrooms," says Patricia Cook, the high school principal. She explained how investments by companies such as IBM and General Electric have helped turn the school around. The corporations provide much needed equipment, and their employees tutor students, serve as role models, and give advice.

Ms. Cook leans over the table. "When you see how these kids have been wronged in life. . . ." Her voice drops off. "I want to give them the best education possible. We require four years of math and science. Next year we start Japanese." Her eyes fairly burn, this young blond educator, born in the Bronx and educated at Vassar. When the bells ring here, students hurry to class. "I want this to be one of the best prep schools in the world," she says.

Throughout Community School District No. 4, which lies entirely within the barrio, things are looking up. In 1974 the district ranked last in citywide reading scores. By 1988 East Harlem students had climbed to 17th place, just above the average. The private investments help, but the district has also pioneered in schools of choice, under which East Harlem junior high youths can enroll in any of 20 "theme schools" in the district. These schools specialize in one area of study: music, computers, science, and so on.

At Public School 83 proud students stood in front of their exhibits on tooth decay, snails, electricity, water pollution, frogs.

Migdalia Maldonado-Torres, the school administrator, turned to Armandi Muniz, 11, and asked a question: "What do you want to be when you grow up?"

"A scientist," he said, eyes bright.

Lizette Santiago was next: "A veterinarian and an actress," she answered, poised and serious in her white blouse and blue skirt.

"I grew up in East Harlem," said Mrs. Maldonado-Torres. "I live in Westchester County now, but I feel a commitment here." She paused. "It's not for the paycheck."

Though they know the odds, people still choose to live in the barrio. Raphael Flores is in that category.

When I first saw Raphael, he was on the phone at Hot Line Cares, the neighborhood's only 24-hour crisis counseling center. He is its director and founder.

He gently chided a caller: "We don't

have time to dance! You have to clean your insides of the hurt, your anger, and the habit."

The doorbell rang, and a waif-like young woman walked in, trying to smile. Warren, a former street kid who works as a volunteer, filled out a form for her.

"I don't know where I live," she said tentatively. "I . . . I would like to seek some help. I don't have nobody to talk to."

"What about drugs?" Warren asked.

"I've been off crack for a week," she said.

Warren made some calls. The rehabilitation centers were full, but she could sleep here until they found a place. She smiled.

When Raphael had a moment, the two of us stepped outside. "There are so many young people like that," he said. "I talk to them about God, tell them they can't do it by themselves. I read them the Bible. It's the only answer I know."

I thought about the people I had met: Roberto, shot; Therese, now in prison for selling heroin; José, negotiating the treacherous currents of the crack trade. But there was also the tenacious Maria, still making dresses and money at her shop; Sister Judy, walking up another flight of stairs to visit another young mother; Alejandro, philosophizing as he clipped another customer's hair; Raphael, trying to save the lost kids; Luz, watching over her daughter. And there was Steven Sloan.

"Come on," Sloan said, "don't drag now." I looked up and saw him, a black man striding ahead of a dozen youngsters. Sloan tapped the ground with a long white cane, feeling his way. When the blind man stopped in the park, the children stopped with him.

"Stretch easy now," Sloan said. "Make sure your legs are straight." He touched their backs and legs with his hand.

"OK, everybody run a lap," said Sloan, a physical education teacher who works with learning disabled youths at Public School 102.

One by one the students straggled back after running their laps on the concrete oval in Jefferson Park.

"I try to teach the kids that life is hard, life is tough, nothing comes easy," Sloan told me. "I try to teach them character, to be proud of what they are."

He made them do sprints again and again. I found myself watching a slender boy, about 14, running ahead of the others. He had a nice easy stride; he could be good.

8

HOME FROM AFAR

There are many kinds of houses, but few creatures have made homes for themselves inside of a book. For this ladybug, however, the book suits her perfectly, especially the pages about gardens. Still, there is something missing . . .

Ladybug's Garden

By Ethel Pochocki
Artwork by Irene Haas

There was once a young ladybug who lived in an old bookstore inside a book called *The English Flower Garden*. She had not planned to live here, but because of the sudden, sad circumstance of losing her parents, it was the best she could do.

She had been quite happy living with her parents high on the shelf in their winter home of *Webster's International Unabridged Dictionary*. Here she had spent happy days becoming a well-educated ladybug and had, right up to the tragic moment, already memorized 122 word definitions.

But then the terrible thing happened: the dictionary was sold, and the ladybug's parents went out of her life forever. She herself had slipped out of the book, sliding down on the letter tabs, and was waiting on the shelf for them. But they never came. They were gone forever.

The book that sat next to the dictionary was almost as fat and heavy. It seemed safe and comfortable. Its edges were quite worn and the lettering faded, but the ladybug could still read the title: *The English Flower Garden*. She crawled up onto the front cover, then over the top edge into the book itself. Fortunately, the cover was loose, so she could travel easily within the pages.

Before she knew it, she found herself on the table of contents and she began to read: "Castle Gardens," "Cottage Gardens," "Bog Gardens," "Alpine Climbers," "Flowering Shrubs"—why, this could be a lovely home! She could learn about the flowers her parents had once promised she would someday see. And there were pictures, she discovered excitedly, drawings of the gardens and forests and terraced castles and thatched-roof cottages.

Slowly her sadness wore away as she

traveled the gardens of England page by page. One day she sat amidst the primroses and Canterbury bells of Fillingham Castle, the next in a cottage garden of hollyhocks at Winchfield, Hants. Another day the ladybug sat under palm trees on the Cornwall coast, and she rang foxglove bells in Somersetshire. Each day brought its own adventure.

Although she learned their names and where they grew, the ladybug could not truly know the flowers, for all the pictures were in black and white. And she couldn't smell them, only read their descriptions and imagine their sweetness or sharpness as she imagined their color. She knew she lived in a black-and-white world that was not the real thing. Still, it was what she had, and she was grateful for it.

The ladybug might have spent her life pleasantly within these pages if the book had not been sold. One day a woman put her gloved hand around *The English Flower Garden* and lifted it from the shelf.

"Oh, I can't believe this," she cried softly. "I've been searching for years for a copy. My grandmother had one, and I remember visiting her and sitting in a swing and reading all about the flowers in Lady So-and-So's garden! I'm *so* happy to find it!"

I'm very happy for you, thought the ladybug, but what's going to happen to me?

The bookseller wrapped the book up. For the moment, the ladybug was safe, but what would happen when the woman began flipping through the pages, reliving her childhood memories page by page? The ladybug could become homeless—or worse—in a matter of seconds.

When the woman arrived home, she put on the tea kettle and began to peel away the brown paper with shaky fingers. She sat down in the rocker by the window and laid the book carefully in her lap. She opened it to the table of contents and she began to smile and sigh. It was just as she remembered it. Meanwhile, the ladybug was safe and snug within Chapter XL: "Alpine Flowers, Rock and Wall Gardens."

Then came a flash of black-and-white fur, surprising the woman. She shrieked and dropped the book.

"Drat you, Max!" the woman muttered angrily to the cat, who hissed and growled back at her. "Look what you've done. If any pages of this precious book have come loose, you'll be punished." The cat looked past her as if she were not there and began to wash his ears.

The woman poured her tea, picked up the book, and sat down once more in the rocker. The ladybug, shaken loose from her rock garden, had fallen deep into the pile of a rug patterned with swirls and scrolls of ivy and flowers. For a moment, she thought she had been dropped into a garden, the colors were so rosy warm and bright. But no, it couldn't be, for all the flowers smelled the same—musty and not too pleasant. She started to follow a scroll as if it were a path, when she felt a dark shadow fall over the rug-flowers. It was Max, coming toward her in a quiet crouch.

He was a young-enough cat to think anything that moved—a mouse, a leaf, a bug—was an enemy to be chased and caught. He came close enough for her to count his whiskers and then he sprang. In her fright, the ladybug spread her wings and flew blindly into the air. This was her first flight, and her sense of direction poor, which is why she landed on the cat's back.

Max was furious. He couldn't see behind him, but he knew something was walking down his spine onto his tail. He danced around and around until the ladybug grew so dizzy, she couldn't hold on. Once again she flew up in awkward circles and landed on an herb wreath hanging on the wall.

She caught her breath, resting for a moment on a sprig of faded lavender. She knew these plants, the silver sage and pearly everlasting of the meadows, and she liked the faintly woodsy smell. But there was a dust-and-brittle feel to them all, with as little life as the black-and-white drawings. No, she thought sadly, this might have been a garden, but it was a very dead one now and it didn't suit her.

Max had disappeared into the kitchen and was trying to get into the silverware drawer, which the woman had left open. The ladybug crawled down the wallpaper of roses

and peonies onto the fireplace mantel, over pictures in silver frames, down the bricks of the fireplace, and back onto the floor.

Then she smelled something so sweet, it almost hurt her to breathe. It was coming from the top of a table by the window where the sun was streaming in. The ladybug flew up and landed in a saucer. Could it be the tea, she wondered? She made her way around the rim of the teacup carefully—one slip and she would find out if she could float or not—but the tea's fragrance, although pleasant, was not what she had smelled.

She scurried, at her ladybug pace, to the blue china bowl sitting at the edge of the table by the window and scaled the side, which was quite slippery. When she reached the top, she gasped.

Here was a garden to rival any in the book! On a bed of water and white pebbles and periwinkle shells sat three bulbs wrapped tightly in their dowdy brown shawls. Their long stringy roots had settled down to the bottom of the bowl, where the shells sang softly of their lost ocean home. From the hearts of the bulbs grew tall green stems topped with heads of frilly red petals. They towered above the ladybug as did the palm trees of the Cornwall coast.

And, oh, the smell! She crawled up each stem and went into the scarlet tendrils until she felt quite drunk and had to come down to rest in their shade.

She was at that moment utterly content in her garden of red hyacinths. At last, she was mistress of a real garden of quiet stream and pebbled path and petaled trees. Here she would bask in the sun and see beyond the window to the blue sky and the chestnut tree and the spirals of mint and sweet peas just breaking through the earth. Perhaps someday, when the window was opened . . . But for now, she asked no more.

Oh, she would have enjoyed the company of her parents or another ladybug, but one couldn't have everything.

The Bakers have uncovered a chain-rattling ghost story set in Athens of long ago. It seems that for as long as there have been storytellers of other times, other habitations, and other glories, there have been spirits to haunt their living rooms, and their tales.

A Haunted House

By Charles F. Baker and Rosalie Baker

What would you do if suddenly one evening a ghost appeared before you in your own home? What if the ghost continued to appear every night?

Almost two thousand years ago, in the land of Italy, a Roman named Pliny wrote a letter to a friend about a ghost who had done just that . . . .

My dear Sura,

I must tell you about Athenodorus and his encounter with a ghost.

It seems that in Greece, in the great city of Athens, there was a large and spacious mansion for sale. The owners had suddenly moved out and put the house on the market at a very low price. Athenodorus, a well-known and highly respected Greek philosopher, chanced to walk by one day and immediately fell in love with the house. Yet he hesitated to buy it, for the price seemed too low. Surely, it is worth more, he thought. I must speak to the owners.

The owners, anxious to sell, yet aware of the fame of Athenodorus, decided to tell him the dreadful secret.

"Our house is haunted. A ghost lives in it. Night after night when we lived there, we heard the sound of iron and the clanging of chains coming closer and closer. Then the ghost would appear, a thin, filthy old man with a ragged beard and shaggy hair. Around his ankles were shackles, and around his wrists chains. At first we took turns watching for him, but after several weeks we were all so afraid that no one could sleep. Finally we abandoned the house to the ghost. We placed a low value on the property, hoping to rid ourselves of it quickly, but we haven't succeeded."

Athenodorus listened closely to this frightful tale. "I would like to rent your house. I'll pay you more than the selling price! Agreed?"

The owners could not believe their ears. Rent? they thought. At an even higher price than we asked? He must be insane! "Yes, yes, we agree," they said out loud.

That evening Athenodorus prepared to meet the ghost. Near the front door he set up a bed, a table with writing materials, and a light so that he might work while he waited.

Night came, and darkness filled the house. All was quiet. Athenodorus could hear only his own breathing. Then, from a distance, came the sound of iron clanging and chains rattling. Athenodorus continued working. Gradually, the noise grew louder as it came closer and closer. Athenodorus sensed the ghost crossing the threshold into his room.

There, just by the door, stood an old, old man in chains. He motioned with a curved finger for Athenodorus to follow him. Still perfectly calm, Athenodorus refused to move. "I have too much work to do. You must wait if you want me to follow you."

The ghost did not accept such an answer. He slowly walked toward Athenodorus, who had returned to his writing. This time the old man rattled his chains above Athenodorus's head and again motioned for him to come. Athenodorus did not refuse. He took his light and followed the thin figure. The ghost, weighed down by the chains, dragged himself slowly into the open courtyard of the house and then suddenly disappeared. Athenodorus stood still—stunned. "Where did he go? Why did he call me? He must have had a reason. Let me mark the spot with some twigs and leaves."

The next day Athenodorus approached the city officials and asked them to come and dig up the courtyard area. They agreed.

Not far beneath the twigs and leaves, the diggers found bones completely entangled in chains. Whose they were or what the story was, no one knew. But it was certain that the poor man had suffered a tragic death and had not been properly buried. Ever since, he had haunted the house, hoping to convince someone to follow him and uncover his terrible secret. Brave Athenodorus had, and after a proper funeral service for the old man, the ghost was never seen again.

Your friend,

Pliny

The original author of this ghost story was a Roman known to us as Pliny the Younger. He was born around A.D. *61 and died about* A.D. *112. Pliny held several public offices, but his favorite occupation was writing and receiving letters, many of which he kept, edited, and published in book form. From reading his letters we find out much about the ancient Greeks and Romans. From his letter to Sura, we know that the Greeks strongly believed in proper burials. If a person died and was not properly buried, that person's spirit would return to haunt its former home and relatives until someone finally performed the proper rites.*

9

VIEWS FROM THE HIGH GROUND

It would be nice if everyone could camp-out on the top of the Empire State Building, but so far, it's only open to Scout troops. Nevertheless, it's an adventure—like sleeping on top of a mountain equipped with high speed elevators.

Empire State Building Camp-Out a Hit

By Diane Leicht

Want to camp at the top of the Empire State Building? Each November, one Scout troop is invited for an overnight camp-out in the observatory of the famous skyscraper. The Rev. Frank Rafter, who began the program in 1963, hosts the visiting troop on a guided tour of the building.

All American and international Boy Scout troops are eligible. Write a letter describing troop activities, civic interests, and the reason why your troop wishes to participate. Send the letter to Empire State Building Management Office, Attn: Boy Scout Camp-out, 350 Fifth Avenue, New York, NY 10118. Building officials pick the lucky troop from the letters they receive.

It may be lonely at the top, but it's also dirty. People who camp and hike haven't always been careful with their mountains, and now we're all paying the price. This newsbrief appeared in the October 1989 National Geographic.

Tidying the World's Highest Trash Pit

Liz Nichol and Bob McConnell went to Mount Everest in 1987 as part of an expedition that came within a thousand feet of the summit via a North Face route. They will return next summer—not to climb up, but to clean up.

Filled with shame that mountaineers have created the "world's highest trash pit," Nichol and McConnell will lead a month-long expedition to the advance base camp, at 18,500 feet, on the Tibetan side of Everest. They will gather trash that has been left by climbers, burn what can be burned on the world's highest mountain, and separate the rest to be carried out and buried or recycled.

The Everest Environmental Expedition, based in Colorado Springs, Colorado, hopes to enlist the cooperation of Tibetans in properly disposing of trash and preserving the area's beauty. It also will work to remind climbers worldwide to carry out their trash and waste. The effort has the support of the American Alpine Club, the Explorers Club, and the American Mountain Foundation.

The view from a high bridge is just a little tidier for wilderness visitors, due to the efforts of the Boy Scout troop featured in this article. You may be surprised just what that skunk is up to, and how without it, the troop just wouldn't be able to do its job.

Take a Skunk to Camp

By William B. McMorris

Photograph by George Olson

"EEEE-YOW!"

The sound echoed off the steep banks of the Noyo River. It shivered among the redwoods that towered nearly 200 feet above the stream.

Was it the yowl of Sasquatch, the legendary man-beast of the dense coastal forests? Was it the screech of the whistle from the nearby railroad?

Neither one. It was just Garrett Alto and Eric Phillips trying to swim in the icy northern California river in the first week of March.

Everybody in Troop 49 knew it was too cold to swim. Eric and Jason Butler laughed so hard they almost dropped their fishing rods. Scoutmaster Scott Butler grinned as Garrett and Eric bounded out of the chilly water. The two quickly toweled themselves off and got into warm, dry clothes.

"We've been swimming here in December," Mr. Butler said, "but it's colder today than it was then."

Cold it was. Cold enough to make Sasquatch, or "Bigfoot" as he is often called, grateful for the thick, shaggy hair that covers his body. The thermometer had dropped into the low 30's the night before. Drafts through the open cabins of Camp Noyo had driven all the Scouts deep within their sleeping bags. Only the smell of bacon and pancakes prepared over two-burner stoves by the patrol cooks the next morning coaxed them out.

Troop 49, chartered to the Ukiah, Calif., First Ward, Church of Jesus Christ of Latter-day Saints, often visits Camp Noyo. The site was once the camp for all Scouts in the Sonoma-Mendocino Area Council in California. The council outgrew the camp, but the Ukiah Scouts still go to Noyo for troop camp-outs.

There's canoeing, fishing and swimming (sometimes) in the river, great campsites amid huge redwoods and Douglas fir, and a choice of pitching tents or bunking in the few remaining cabins.

Another part of going to Camp Noyo is the chance to ride the "Skunk Train." No, not a train that hauls skunks, but the Cali-

Diesel Skunk M-300 rumbles by as Scouts clean a shelter. Cars like this one stop for people anywhere on the line.

fornia Western train that runs along the course of the Noyo River. The engines, especially the self-propelled diesel cars that run like huge buses on train wheels, won the nickname "Skunks" because of their fumes. Local residents say, "You can smell 'em before you see 'em."

The little trains rumble across 40 miles of the most twisty rails in America. They wind through a redwood forest, dive through two tunnels dug by Chinese laborers nearly 100 years ago, and criss-cross the Noyo River on 31 trestles.

Begun as a logging railroad in 1885, the line now hauls sightseers and freight between Fort Bragg on the Pacific shore to Willits, beyond the coastal hills. "It's really fun," said Jared Shipee. "And the tracks run right by camp."

Scouts can toss their backpacks aboard a Skunk, ride at special fares, enjoy the winding trip through the redwoods and step off the train into the camp. Once at Noyo, they are in wilderness. The only other way to get to this area is on logging roads that are rough, dangerous and sometimes impassable. When you go to Camp Noyo, it is one time when taking a Skunk to camp makes sense.

Troop 49 has always found Camp Noyo a great place for service projects too.

On this weekend camp-out, the troop put handrail covers on a suspension bridge that spans the Noyo at the point where it cuts through the middle of camp. The wooden rails had weathered until anyone reaching out to balance himself on the swaying bridge stood a good chance of grabbing a handful of splinters.

Troop 49 split old sections of fire hose and nailed them in place over the rails to cover the rough wood. They also improved a path down to the outlet of a clear running spring.

Across the Noyo, Brian Christensen, the troop guide, was directing his patrol of new Scouts as they cleaned up campsites and the sheltered platform that stands beside the railroad tracks. He had volunteered for the job of helping the new boys learn Scouting skills.

"Hey! Bigfoot tracks!" Chris Thompson pointed at the ground and pretended to be amazed.

"Naw, those are Brian's," Bobby Walker said. The rest of the patrol laughed and Brian grinned.

"Just keep busy," he told the gagsters.

Brian, 17, was the former senior patrol leader of the troop. Even though he might have looked as large as Bigfoot to some of the younger Scouts, they respected him more for his easy manner and his patience than his size.

By late morning a steady, cold rain chilled the hands and trickled down the necks of the Scouts, but the work continued. The bridge rails were covered, campsites and platform cleaned, and the path to the spring was finished.

Mr. Butler gave the word to pack and head for the railroad platform.

By midafternoon they gave up life in the dripping woods for a warm, dry seat in a Skunk Train passenger car. A humming diesel locomotive took them back through the forest to town and their rides home. Once again they had proved it was fun to go camping with a Skunk.

10

THE VIEW FROM THE FIELD (SOME OF THE YEAR'S EVENTS)

Two of the most frightening events of 1989 were the San Francisco earthquake and Hurricane Hugo, which ripped across the Caribbean and through North and South Carolina. Sam Chu Lin reports:

Earthquake! Hurricane! Scouts on Both Coasts Aid Survivors

By Sam Chu Lin

5:04 P.M., Oct. 17, 1989—Game 3 of the World Series is about to get under way at San Francisco's Candlestick Park. The packed stadium begins to shake. Pieces of concrete fall from the stands.

Meanwhile, in San Francisco's Marina district, gas lines rupture, setting fire to homes and apartments. Black columns of smoke fill the sky.

As commuters drive home from work, part of the top deck of the San Francisco–Oakland Bay Bridge collapses. It falls to the lower deck, trapping two cars.

In Oakland, a mile-long section of two-tiered Interstate 880 falls, crushing vehicles on the lower level like a giant stepping on aluminum cans.

In counties farther south, hundreds of homes and buildings are knocked off their foundations or made uninhabitable. A shopping mall is ruined.

Cause of the destruction: an earthquake measuring 7.1 on the Richter scale. The quake lasted 15 seconds. Though not the "big one" predicted to hit California, it was the worst to hit the city since 1906. The 1989 quake killed at least 67 people and caused an estimated $5.8 billion in damage. In an instant, hundreds of people lost their homes and possessions.

Policemen, firemen and emergency medical crews rushed into action. And throughout the Bay Area, the Boy Scouts of America did its part to help:

- Cub Scouts collected food and clothing for the Salvation Army to distribute in the Marina district.
- Explorers manned telephones at the

Oakland police station, taking calls for missing persons.

- While rescue teams searched for survivors under the collapsed I-880, Boy Scouts handed out food to workers and residents.

One of the hardest-hit communities was Watsonville, south of San Francisco. Twelve hundred people were made homeless. Many had to live in tents.

Scouts and parents from Troop 463 of Sunnyvale collected and distributed food and supplies for Watsonville's homeless and worked at a disaster relief center.

Many of the Sunnyvale Scouts were shocked at the damage they saw.

"I've seen pictures of the earthquake devastation many times on television," said Life Scout Ken McAfee of Troop 463, "but you don't really know what it's like until you see it in person."

Scouts helped set up a day-care facility. They delivered food, medical supplies, and clothing to a campsite for farm workers. Several Scout mothers helped treat children hit with an outbreak of chicken pox.

"When we unloaded the van, there were long lines to get the supplies," said Eagle Scout Mark Chu Lin of Troop 463. "The people really needed help!"

Many other Scouting units have helped quake victims. For example:

- Cub Scout Pack 139 of Glendale, Calif., adopted a Santa Cruz family and is sending them food certificates.

- Scouts from Troop 41 of San Jose, Calif., raised $3,425 to buy food and supplies.

- When a power outage knocked out traffic signals, Sunnyvale Troop 441 directed traffic. Later, they collected 1,200 pounds of food and 500 pounds of coats and blankets for the homeless.

- Cub Scouts, Boy Scouts and Girl Scouts in the small community of Hartville, Mo., hundreds of miles from San Francisco, collected a truckload of toys, food and furniture.

- Eagle Scout Doug Keehn of Watsonville Troop 599, along with other members of the Order of the Arrow, have encouraged the local Scout council to set up an adopt-a-senior-citizen program.

"We want to make sure seniors are getting food and the necessary assistance," Keehn said.

Scouts will continue to help as long as help is needed. BSA officials say the Scouts' response to the quake illustrates "the best in Scouting's ideals."

Lesson From the Quake: Be Prepared

An earthquake occurs when pieces of the earth's crust, called plates, slide past each other along a fault line.

The October quake released only a fraction of the energy built up along the 800-mile-long San Andreas fault in California.

According to experts, the San Francisco Bay area has at least a 20 percent likelihood of suffering a major earthquake within the next 30 years. In some areas along the San Andreas fault, the likelihood is as high as 90 percent.

If the big quake hits, strict building codes and well-planned rescue operations will save thousands of lives. But experts say still more planning and preparation are needed.

VINCENT MAGGIORA/SAN FRANCISCO CHRONICLE

Shock waves from the earthquake turned the mud base of San Francisco's Marina District into mush, tossing houses off their foundations and into the streets.

After October's quake, a local phone company published a full-page newspaper ad in San Francisco that encouraged area residents to "learn from the Boy Scouts" and "Be Prepared."

Hurricane Hugo

San Francisco's earthquake wasn't the only major disaster last fall. On Sept. 21 and 22, Hurricane Hugo struck the Carolinas after ripping through several islands in the Caribbean.

Hugo devastated entire communities. Tens of thousands of people were left homeless; a third of South Carolina's forests fell. Damage estimates totaled $4 billion, making Hugo the most costly storm ever to hit the U.S. mainland.

Scouts went to work immediately. They collected food, clothing, and bottled water for the homeless. Dozens of Scouting units from several different councils did community service projects.

"Wherever there were food supplies [being offered], there were long lines waiting for them," said Jerry Wilburn, a leader of Troop 411 of Doraville, Ga. That troop delivered supplies to Summerville, S.C., where Hugo spawned numerous tornadoes.

"Trees were twisted and blown down in piles," Mr. Wilburn said. "The sound of chain saws and the smell of fresh cut wood were everywhere."

Scouting units doing Good Turns will stay busy for months to come.

Every 10 years, the United States takes a headcount. It sounds so simple. Robert Bahr discovered that it's not. You may sympathize, but you might also laugh at this article, published in 1990—a census year.

Counting Noses

By Robert Bahr

Illustrated by John Huehnergarth

"You want me to climb a *what*?"

Bill Smith was 22 years old, just out of college and needed a job.

"They're hiring people to take the census," one of his friends told him. "Easy work. Nothing to it." So Bill applied.

His first assignment: to interview a man living on top of a flagpole.

Once every 10 years, people like Bill try to get in touch with every home in the United States.

This year is a census year. In April, your family should have received a list of questions in the mail. If you didn't mail back the answers, a census taker probably came to your home in person. The job is not as easy as it sounds.

For example, during the last census, in 1980, a worker had to be flown into the forest wilderness of northern Minnesota by Coast Guard helicopter. He needed to check out the population of a few log cabins.

"There were more moose and wolves in the territory than humans," he found.

A young woman had to interview a couple living on a mountain in Nevada. A heavy April snowfall had trapped the people in their home for several days.

That didn't stop the census taker. She borrowed a minitractor with Caterpillar tracks and spent half the day chugging up the mountainside to get the job done.

Census takers have used horses, boats, bobsleds, skis and even an aerial tramway to reach the people they have to count.

That's how important the census is. For one thing, the number of representatives your state sends to Congress depends on the size of the state's population.

Suppose a half-million new residents moved into your state over the past 10 years, but no one took a census. The state wouldn't get the additional representatives in the U.S. Congress that it deserves.

What's more, your neighborhood might not get the new schools, parks and playgrounds it needs.

Government agencies also need to know in which areas people are out of work, so that they can encourage new jobs. They have to find the homeless so that they can build new housing in the right areas.

That's the kind of information Bill Smith set out to gather in Atlanta, Ga., on a sunny April morning four censuses ago—in 1950. He just never expected to get it from a

USA
Huehnergarth
Huehnergarth

man living on an 8-by-5-foot platform 60 feet above the ground.

Thirty-year-old Odell Smith had been sitting on that flagpole for several months. He had endured winds of 120 miles an hour, strong enough to rip the shirt off his back. Odell was out of work, so he had decided to set a world record in flagpole sitting.

The only way to reach the top was to sit on a flimsy canvas seat that could be hoisted up.

"I could feel that pole swaying," Bill recalls. "But I knew somebody had to talk to this guy. So I gritted my teeth and took the ride."

Half an hour later, Bill Smith returned to earth with the details. "Odell," Bill reported, "is married, has no children, currently lives on a flagpole. His profession—flagpole sitting."

Nobody seems to know what happened to Odell Smith after that, but Bill Smith became a psychiatrist and raised a family.

Just last year, Bill retired. This past April, at age 62, he was out knocking on doors, a census taker again.

"I'm looking forward to it," he said beforehand. "But I'll tell you one thing. I'm not climbing any flagpoles this time around!"

This piece appeared in a November 17, 1989 issue of the newspaper for schools, Current Events. *We'd like to know what the townspeople ate for dinner that day, after the rain.*

A Fishy Story

Illustration by John Gibson

You've heard the expression, "It's raining cats and dogs." Well, in Australia recently it rained *fishes.* No kidding. In Ipswich, a small town about 30 miles from Australia's coast, people looked up to actually see large amounts of squirming fish falling from the sky! The fish were sardines.

Meteorologists think that a waterspout probably lifted the sardines from water along the coast and deposited them inland.

Waterspouts are whirling funnels of air and mist that form over water. The powerful suction caused by a waterspout draws water—along with the many creatures that live in it—up into the sky.

Scientists say waterspouts seem to sort out the animals according to weight and shape before depositing them on the Earth. On rare occasions, the entire animal population of a lake or pond may be deposited in one area. This happened in Essex, England, many years ago.

It rained fishes in Australia.

11

GAMES, GOOFING OFF, AND DOWNRIGHT FIBBING

If this story looks sort of familiar, but not really, it's because it's a "fractured" or lied-about fairytale. The author takes a well-known story and makes it his own with additions and changes. It forces readers to think about two *stories at once—the one they know, and the new one. Now that you know the trick, go out and fracture a few tales of your own!*

Little Green Riding Hood

By Gianni Rodari

Illustrations by Walter Lorraine

ONCE UPON A TIME there was a little girl called Little Yellow Riding Hood."

"No! *Red* Riding Hood!"

"Oh yes, of course, Red Riding Hood. Well,

one day her mother called and said: 'Little Green Riding Hood—' "

"Sorry! Red. 'Now, my child, go to Aunt Mary and take her these potatoes.' "

"No! It doesn't go like that! 'Go to Grandma and take her these cakes.' "

"All right. So the little girl went off and in the wood she met a giraffe."

"What a mess you're making of it! It was a wolf!"

"And the wolf said: 'What's six times eight?' "

"No! No! The wolf asked her where she was going."

"So he did. And Little Black Riding Hood replied—"

"Red! Red!! Red!!!"

"She replied: 'I'm going to the market to buy some tomatoes.' "

"No, she didn't. She said: 'I'm going to my grandma who is sick, but I've lost my way.' "

"Of course! And the horse said—"

"What horse? It was a wolf."

"So it was. And this is what it said: 'Take the 75 bus, get out at the main square, turn right, and at the first doorway you'll find three steps. Leave the steps where they are, but pick up the dime you'll find lying on them, and buy yourself a packet of chewing gum.' "

"Grandpa, you're terribly bad at telling stories. You get them all wrong. But all the same, I wouldn't mind some chewing gum."

"All right. Here's your dime." And the old man turned back to his newspaper.

If we told you about a club just for liars, would you believe us? If you're capable of telling the most outrageous stories around, you may already be a member.

Championship Whoppers from the Liars Club

By Nino Lo Bello

Illustrated by John Huehnergarth

Scouts should never lie. But everyone enjoys hearing a good tall tale. Here are some award winners.

Mark Twain, the famous writer who once piloted steamboats on the Mississippi River, claimed one time he counted 136 kinds of weather along the river in 24 hours. Fibs like that helped Twain earn a reputation as one of America's best tellers of tall tales.

Twain died in 1910, but if he were alive today, the author of *The Adventures of Tom Sawyer* and *The Adventures of Huckleberry Finn* would probably belong to the Burlington Liars Club of Burlington, Wis.

The club has a library of lies of which even Twain could be proud. We're not talking about the low-down lies that some people use to fool others. We're talking tall tales, which no one believes but many find amusing.

Every year since 1929, fibbers have mailed their favorite fabrications to Burlington to compete for the Best Lie of the Year award. The liars contest has brought in tall tales by the thousands. Some samples:

"My wife," wrote one man from Texas (who, as it turned out, lied about being married), "is so lazy that she feeds the chickens popcorn, so that the eggs will turn themselves over when she fries them."

Another liar offered this: "My wife has such cold feet that when she takes off her shoes, the furnace goes on and when she gets under the electric blanket, the street-lights go dim."

From Canada: "Up here in Alberta we really have some big windstorms. Last summer a rancher had dug 2,000 post-holes when a strong wind blew the post-holes clean out of the ground. When they were found 125 miles away, they were torn so full of holes from bounding over the cactus that they wouldn't hold any more dirt."

And finally this beaut from Minnesota: "The floods in northern Minnesota were so bad last spring that the turtles climbed out of their shells and used them for rowboats."

Weather is always a popular subject among liars, particularly fog. The best fog yarns to land in Wisconsin so far include these three:

"When I was a kid living in Nova Scotia, fog would get so thick it would fill the house. One evening when Mom turned her back to the stove, the fish she was frying swam away."

"The fog in Los Angeles comes in off the ocean so frequently and so thick that we are considering printing our street signs in Braille."

And this dazzler from Pennsylvania: "The fog was so thick around here last year that when we cut down a tree, it couldn't fall over until the fog lifted."

Burlington, population 9,000, gets lies like these from all over the world. Every December, club directors say, they go through a pile of lies higher than Mt. McKinley. (Don't believe it.) The writer of the winning lie gets a parchment certificate proclaiming him the best liar of the year.

Roy Griesbach of Appleton, Wis., won last year's contest with this lie about the drought of 1988: "The weather was so dry that the only water one could buy was dehydrated in 16-ounce packages."

Lowell Wolfe of Sturgis, Mich., said this about the drought: "Whenever I scaled bluegills, I held them underwater to keep the dust out of my eyes."

A man in Topeka wrote: "Kansas was so dry last summer that bullfrogs born in the spring never learned how to swim."

Several liars sent in this one: "The drought was so bad that the trees were chasing the dogs."

So far, very few women have copped the championship, and no one under 16 has ever won.

But anyone can join the club and give it a try. Write the Burlington Liars Club, Inc., Burlington, WI 53105.

Some lucky people get an honorary membership. For instance, when a columnist in Birmingham, Ala., heard that the club had members in every state except Alabama, he wrote: "What do you expect? There *are* no liars in Alabama." For this, the Liars Club awarded him a free lifetime membership.

Mitzi Robers, the club's secretary-treasurer, believes that women are probably the best liars around. Yet the club did not have its first female winner until the 56th annual competition in 1985. That year, Marie Weatherly of Oklahoma City submitted this winning tale:

"Here in Oklahoma we have very high winds, but two years ago they were higher than usual. The tomatoes in my garden couldn't get ripe because the wind kept blowing the sun off them."

Tales about the wind come in more than any other kind. The big winner a few years ago was about the shepherd who kept a 100-pound sack of flour hanging on the wall outside his door. During the night, the winds came barging in, and the next morning the man found that the sack had been blown away—but the flour was still hanging there.

John Soeth, club president, says the lie entered most often is the one about the man who had only one bullet but was facing two angry bears. The man fired his gun at a knife, which cut the bullet in two, each half killing a bear. Another common tale is about the mosquitoes being so big that screens have to be made from chicken wire.

Common lies like those don't win. So, if you try to fib for fame, improve your chances of winning by inventing a fib of your own.

The poor fellow was up against two angry bears but had only one bullet.

The Liars Club was started by newspaperman Otis C. Hulett. One New Year's Eve, Hulett, working as the Burlington correspondent for the *Racine Journal Times*, made up a story about how the police and firemen of Burlington would get together before the New Year to see who could tell the biggest lies. Hulett wired in a story stating that the chief of police (Frank Beller) won the lying contest by claiming, "I never told a lie in my life."

Surprisingly, the next year the Associated Press called Hulett to see if there would be another champion liar contest. Taken aback, Hulett said, "Sure!" That was the beginning.

Hulett, who died this year at age 91, ran the Liars Club for a half century, building it up to a membership of more than 100,000 people in more than 60 countries.

After tiny Burlington's fame had spread throughout the solar system, Hulett and his cohorts decided to incorporate in 1935. They filled out an application for a charter, but a skeptical Wisconsin state official rejected the initial bid with the following message:

"Do you really mean it, or is this just one of your darned lies?"

So maybe you would give your right ear for an Olympic medal; in long ago Alaska, it wouldn't have been far-fetched. The "Fairbanks Games" tradition goes back 3,000 years, but we're not sure—if you lost your ear, did you win, or lose?

The Champion Ear-Puller Is . . .

Most people are familiar with Olympic events like running and swimming. But did you ever hear of ear-pulling? That's an event at the World Eskimo-Indian Olympics held each summer in Fairbanks, Alaska. These Olympics feature games that have been played by Native Alaskans for more than 3,000 years.

In the Four-Man Carry, four men place their arms around one man's neck, and he carries them as far as he can.

In the Blanket Toss, a person is launched into the air by 40 teammates holding a seal-skin blanket. The person tossed the highest is the winner. Hunters once used this method to spot animals from high in the sky.

In the Ear Pull, two contestants have a tug-of-war. They tug a loop of twine with their ears! They pull until the twine comes off one person's ear. This game tests a person's ability to endure pain. In olden days, some contestants even lost their ears. Ouch!

Several books have been written about what Norman Rockwell was like, but anyone who looks at his pictures knows that he had a quick wit and a playful sense about the country he was part of.

Norman Rockwell: Twentieth-Century Storyteller

Magazines today are full of photographs. From cover to cover, photographs show what is happening across the country and around the world. But a hundred years ago, magazines did not have the technology to reproduce photographs, so they depended on artists to draw and paint the scenes and portraits.

During the second half of the nineteenth century, the number and quality of publications increased, as did the illustrations in them. The era from the 1880s through the 1920s is known as the Golden Age of Illustration. The artists who made their careers as illustrators during that time included some of the best talent in America—Winslow Homer, Frederic Remington, and Howard Pyle, among others.

Norman Rockwell was born in the middle of the Golden Age. As a young boy, he was not very good at playing sports and games, but he discovered that he had a talent for drawing, which he used to entertain his friends. In his early teens, Rockwell knew he wanted to be an artist, and by the age of twenty-two, he had achieved his goal. He was a major-league illustrator painting covers for the *Saturday Evening Post*, one of America's most popular magazines.

Rockwell saw himself as a storyteller who used pictures rather than words. He told his own tales in his many magazine covers and other people's stories in illustrations for books, articles, advertisements, and news events. As Norman Rockwell painted pictures of America, Americans fell in love with him. In the preface to Rockwell's 1960 autobiography, *Post* editor Ben Hibbs wrote, "It is no exaggeration to say simply that Norman Rockwell is the most popular, the most loved, of all contemporary artists. For thirty-nine years, while the face of the world was changing unbelievably, Norman has amused, charmed and inspired a great many millions of Americans. . . . [S]omehow he himself is like a gallery of Rockwell paintings—friendly, human, deeply American, varied in mood, but full, always, of the zest of living."

The story of my life is, really, the story of my pictures and how I made them. Because, in one way or another, everything I have seen and done has gone into my pictures.

—NORMAN ROCKWELL

When Norman Rockwell painted his Triple Self-Portrait *in 1960, he included self-portraits of several other artists pinned to the easel as though for inspiration.*

April Fool's Fun

By Shari Lyn Zuber

After all the hard work that went into creating the "Four Freedoms" illustrations, Norman Rockwell decided to do something lighthearted for the *Saturday Evening Post* cover. The April 3, 1943, cover was the first of three April Fool's Day designs the artist did (the other two were in 1945 and 1948). Called *April Fool: Checkers*, the painting was the artist's answer to the people who wrote to him complaining about the misuse of props in other covers he had drawn.

Norman Rockwell painted forty-five mistakes in the drawing. Look carefully and see how many you can find. Answers on page 162.

THE SATURDAY EVENING
POST
APRIL 3, 1943
10¢
The never-before-told story of our marines' struggle for survival
LAST MAN OFF WAKE ISLAND
By LT. COL. W. L. J. BAYLER, USMC
NORMAN ROCKWELL'S APRIL-FOOL COVER SEE PAGE 4

Answers to April Fool's Fun from page 160.

Easier Mistakes

Fish on stairway
Water on stairway
Mailbox in house
Faucet at side of fireplace
Wallpaper pattern behind faucet upside-down
Woodpecker pecking woman's chair
Mushrooms growing out of carpet
Woman's dress has back pocket
Newspaper in her pocket
Small silhouette pictures on wall hung upside-down
Scissors used as candleholders
Plate of bacon and egg on mantelpiece
Clock on mantel has April Fool for numbers
Portraits have man coming out of picture
Mouse's head popping out of mantelpiece
Two ducks flying across scene
Crown on woman's head
Skunk on woman's lap
Woman has a wrench for a nutcracker in her hand
Woman wearing pants under her dress
Woman wearing ice skates
Glass and medicine bottle floating in air
Wallet attached to string, which is attached to man's finger
Bird in man's pocket
Man wearing a dress
Man wearing roller skates
Man has hoe for a cane
Deer under man's chair
Plants growing out of the carpet
Milk bottles growing out of plants
Zebra looking out of picture frame
Artist's signature backward

Difficult Mistakes

Fishhook in front of fish on stairway
Stairway behind fireplace (Rockwell claimed this was architecturally impossible)
Two different patterns on wallpaper
Buttons on wrong side of woman's sweater
Woman's wedding ring on wrong hand
Wrong number of squares on checkerboard
No checkers on checkerboard
Pencil behind man's ear has eraser on both ends
Tire is rim of fireplace
Fork instead of spoon on top of medicine bottle
Too many fingers on man's hand
Buckle on man's slipper
Deer has dog's paws

It's no April Fool's joke—flea circuses are real. Sallie Luther writes about the tiniest three-ring circuses in the world, and the hard-working bugs slugging out a living as performers.

The Smallest Show on Earth

By Sallie Luther

Photograph by Nicole Duplaix

"LADIES AND GENTLEMEN, boys and girls, the circus is about to begin! You've heard about it, you've read about it, and now here it is—before your very eyes! Step right up! Get your popcorn, your peanuts, your magnifying glass!"

Hold it, *you're probably saying.* A magnifying glass? *That's right—because this circus is a bit on the small side. In fact, it's a* flea *circus!*

Flea circuses have been around for hundreds, maybe thousands, of years. They are rare to day. But in the "old days," many traveled from town to town or fair to fair.

The audience would gather around a barrel top or small table. There the fleas pulled tiny chariots and carriages. They circled round and round on flea-powered carousels and ferris wheels. They even "kicked" miniature footballs!

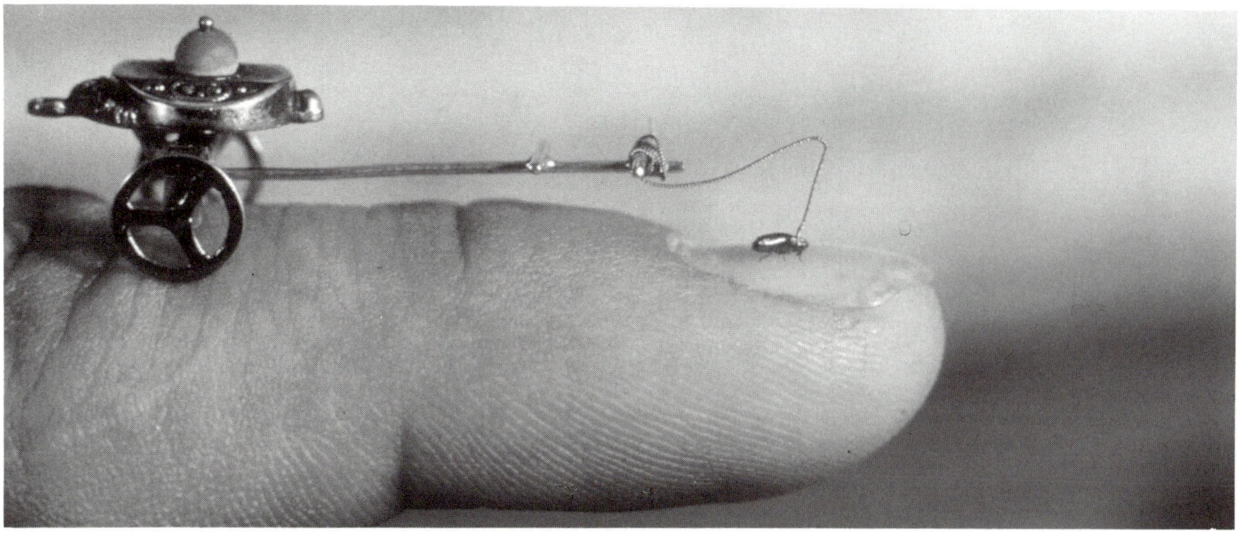

Between performances, the speck-sized superstars lived in snug little cotton-filled chests, drawers, or boxes. They dined on their favorite food—fresh blood from the arm or leg of a human "trainer."

Now I'm sure some of you are asking: *How did anyone train a flea?* The answer is that no one did—not really. Fleas try to hide from light. So when they were brought out to "perform," they hopped and scurried and scrambled around, struggling to escape. But thin wires harnessed the fleas and kept them captive. The fleas' actions made the show go.

Could you see a live flea circus today? There are still a few in Europe. But, sadly, nearly all of the tiny flea tents have folded.

There's an old saying in show business: The show must go on. Wouldn't it be fun if you could just borrow some "performers" from a pet cat or dog? And wouldn't it be fun to set up a modern-day flea circus? Then again, maybe it wouldn't. Most people aren't too crazy about having fleas in their house—not even "trained" circus fleas!

If this game was so popular and fun, why do the players look so grim? Perhaps because once they had gambled away their jewelry and other precious objects, they were playing for their freedom. The loss of freedom could last a lifetime—but still the game endured.

Patolli: A Game of Ancient Mexico

By Harry Gardiner

Illustrated by Coni Porter

One of the most popular games played in ancient Mexico during the Postclassical period (A.D. 1200 to 1521) was *patolli.* This gambling game, originally played by the Aztecs, was named after the unusual two-sided dice made from large, flat beans called *patoles.* According to one writer, patolli was especially popular among peasants, who played for jewelry, precious stones, blankets, and other objects. When they had nothing left to bet, they sometimes played for themselves at fixed prices. Losers agreed to be lifelong slaves of the winner unless they could buy back their freedom within a stated period of time.

Patolli has been compared to the modern games of backgammon and Parcheesi. It is still played, in various forms and under different names, by Indian tribes in remote areas of Mexico.

The Board

The board or playing field originally consisted of a mat made from palm leaves. Players drew a square on the mat and painted two diagonal and crossed lines within it. These lines were then divided into squares, or houses. The two crossed arms of the board shown are of equal length and contain two

rows of eight squares each. The four squares in the middle of the board represent a safe place where opponents cannot attack. The board consists of a total of 68 squares.

The Players

The game is usually played by two people, although several players can make up two teams.

The Dice

Each of four two-sided bean-shaped dice is marked on one side with the numbers 1, 2, 3, or 4 and is blank on the other side. Coins with numbers taped to them make a good substitute for these dice.

Moves are determined by the combination of numbers appearing on the dice when they are thrown. Two dice with the numbered sides up = 2. Three dice with the numbered sides up = 3. Four dice with the numbered sides up = 4. Four dice with the numbered sides down = 5. If only one numbered die faces up, 1 = 1, 2 = 10, 3 = 15, and 4 = 20.

The Game

The object of the game is for a player to move six red or blue pieces around his or her T-shaped course before an opponent can do the same. Red and blue poker chips, colored buttons, or coins of different denominations make good playing pieces. Since play with this many pieces can get very complicated, you might want to start with only three pieces.

To decide who goes first, both players toss the four dice. The one with the highest score places one playing piece on his or her starting square and tosses the dice again to begin play.

Whenever a player's first piece lands on or passes one of the black triangles shown on the board, that player may enter another piece at the original starting square. Players then toss the dice once for each piece in play. For example, if you have three pieces in play and make throws of 4, 10, and 2, you might move the first piece 10 places, the second 4, and the third 2.

When one player lands on a square occupied by the other player, the second player's piece is "eaten," or removed from the board. It may be reentered only when that player's first piece lands on or passes a black triangle. As before, it begins at the starting square. Pieces are safe from being eaten on the four center squares, which may be occupied by both players at the same time and by any number of pieces.

A player's piece enters the "exiting ramp" when it lands on the part of the board where play first began. Once there, throws of 10, 15, or 20 count only as 1. Pieces exit when they land on the starting square. Although these pieces are no longer in play, the player may still throw for them. For example, if one piece has exited and two are still in play, the player may throw three times, using these numbers in any combination to move the two pieces still in play as long as each piece is moved at least once. The first player to move all his or her pieces off the board is the winner.

Trace these shapes on colored paper, then cut them out.

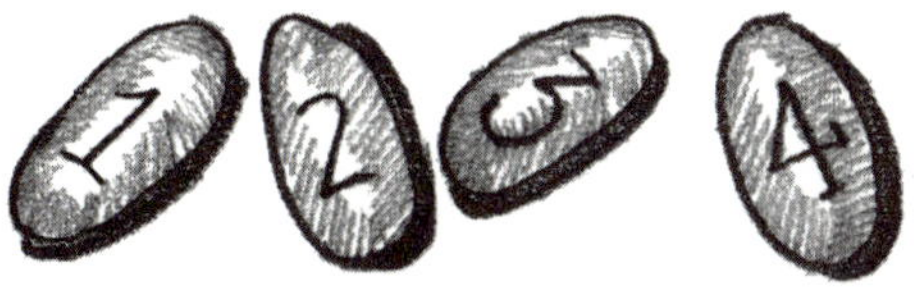

Bean-shaped dice

12

TWELVE O'CLOCK AND ALL IS WELL: THE TIME RIDDLE

It all sounds so confusing, but what it comes down to is this: you can start the 21st century any day you want, as long as you get everyone else to agree to it.

When Does the 21st Century Begin?

The first day of the 21st century will be (A) January 1, 2000; (B) January 1, 2001.

Most people will probably celebrate the beginning of the next *millennium*, or thousand years, on January 1, 2000, says Tim Willard of the World Future Society. However, mathematicians point out that the 21st century begins January 1, 2001. The 20th century ends with its 100th year—the year 2000.

Do not worry if you don't "get" everything in this article, because adults—or White Rabbits—don't either. No matter how much you skip, there's still enough to make your head spin pleasantly or your mind take a wild rollercoaster ride.

The Enigma of Time

By John Boslough

Who better to explain something as elusive as time than Richard P. Feynman. He dominated the physics of his generation, rewrote our understanding of how matter and energy behave, helped develop the atom bomb.

"What is time?" repeated the late Nobel laureate. "We physicists work with it every day, but don't ask me what it is. It's just too difficult to think about."

Recently I saw a graffito on a wall of a café in Austin, Texas, that attempted an answer: "Time is nature's way of keeping everything from happening all at once."

Ask six people to explain time today, and, like the six blind men poking the elephant, you may get six answers. A physicist might say time is one of the two basic building blocks of the universe, the other being space. For a clockmaker time is the ticktock of his handiwork. For a science-fiction fan it is the fourth dimension. A biologist sees time in the internal clocks that keep plants and animals in sync with nature. For a banker it is money, while a Buddhist monk contemplates time in the eternally returning cycles of nature.

"We have given more attention to measuring time than to anything in nature," says Gernot Winkler, Director of Time Services at the U.S. Naval Observatory in Washington, D.C. "But time remains an abstraction, a riddle that exists only in our minds."

Psychologists tell us that children before the age of two have little sense of the passage of time. It may have been the same for our early ancestors. Some scholars believe that people once lived in a state of "timeless present" with little or no sense of past or future.

Julian Jaynes, a Princeton psychologist and author, contends this may have been true as late as the eighth century B.C., when the *Iliad* was first written down. He contends that the epic poem attributed to Homer displays little awareness of time.

According to Jaynes the poem was about people who "did not live in a frame of past happenings, who did not have 'lifetimes' in our sense, and who could not reminisce"—abilities that were acquired only when language advanced to the point that we could describe the past in terms of personal experience.

The way science views time also has changed. Throughout most of history time was looked upon as a flow like a river. Even for the remarkable English scientist Sir

Isaac Newton, the flow of time was absolute. But with the arrival of Albert Einstein's theories of relativity, time was first seen as a dimension—like height and width—giving meaning to events and the order in which they occur. Time, quite literally, was something that keeps everything from happening at once.

Einstein also showed that our perception of time is local, peculiar to our planet. This is because time is affected by the gravitational field of each celestial body, and thus is unique to any one spot in the universe.

Early people presumably first realized time passed when they saw that they lived in a world of constant change. We have come to place a premium on measuring the flow of time—as if by measuring it we could begin to understand it.

Devising accurate calendars and clocks, however, proved to be one of man's most elusive and protracted intellectual pursuits. The long struggle to affix numbers to the passage of time parallels our organizing ourselves in a complex, modern world.

It began in the great civilizations that awakened five millennia ago along the life-giving rivers of the Middle East: in Sumer between the Tigris and Euphrates and in Egypt along the Nile. Drawn like most ancient people to the movements of the heavens and the changing seasons, the Babylonians developed a year of 360 days, then divided it into 12 lunar months of 30 days each. This was not a simple feat, since the sun and moon do not dance in step, the moon's cycles occurring approximately every 29½ days and the earth's every 365¼ days.

Babylonian astronomers knew the true number of days in a year, but kept it at 360

A sculpture of working clocks stands in front of Gare St. Lazere, a railroad station that is used as a central meeting place in the city of Paris, France. This monument to time is by the French Sculptor César.

FRANCO ZECCHIN/MAGNUM

because their priests insisted the number—which may have led to the number of degrees in a circle—possessed magical properties. The practical Egyptians extended the year by five days, which they set aside for feasting during the Nile's annual flooding. Refinements by the Romans and by Pope Gregory XIII in 1582 gave us today's Gregorian calendar, accurate to a day in every 3,323 years.

Early societies also broke the day itself into smaller units, presumably for the same reason as do our clocks and watches—so you know when you're supposed to be somewhere.

The sun, arcing daily across the sky, was undoubtedly the first timepiece, followed perhaps by the shadow of a stick stuck in the ground—a crude sundial to mark the hours.

The time-conscious Egyptians divided the day into two cycles of 12 hours each. Why not eight or ten? The 12-hour division might have come from the numbering system of the Sumerians or from star patterns in the sky.

In the 11th century A.D. a Chinese scholar named Su Song erected a colossal contraption that was among the first mechanical water clocks.

In a Beijing museum I examined a model that did scant justice to the scale of Su Song's creativity. More than 30 feet high, powered by a waterwheel, bristling with shafts and levers, his combination planetarium-clock signaled the quarter hours with gongs, bells, and a sort of glockenspiel. Its crowning feature was a water-triggered device called an escapement that stopped the clock's movement at set intervals, forcing it to run at a steady rate.

Whether Su Song's invention found its way into Europe or evolved there independently, the mechanical clock has achieved its greatest glory in the West.

Forged by an unknown ironsmith, the first mechanical clock in Europe is believed to have been built for an English monastery in the 13th century. It and other early monastery clocks consisted of crude iron gears driven by weights—a kind of reverse windlass—but no dials; initiates were called to prayer by bells, known in Middle English as "cloks."

In Pisa, Italy, I found a lamp that, according to legend, led to more accurate clocks. In the 16th century Galileo Galilei, a young medical student, spied the lantern swinging in a church. Timing it with his pulse, he found that each swing took the same amount of time, regardless of the distance traveled. He had discovered the pendulum. Exhilarated, he gave up medicine to study physics. But seven decades passed before Dutch scientist Christian Huygens build the first pendulum clock, ushering in the era of precision timekeeping.

By the 17th century the clock already was having a profound effect on society. The notion that time is money became an essential ingredient of emerging capitalism. In the early 1800s some mill owners created the mill clock, an insidious device that ran fast or slow according to how hard workers labored.

In those days time zones did not exist, and the world was a hodgepodge of local times. Nor was there a prime meridian where a 24-hour count could begin for all navigators; most used the time at their home ports as they roved the seas.

At an 1884 meeting in Washington, D.C., Britain and the United States urged international adoption of Greenwich, site of the Royal Observatory, as zero-degree longitude. Jerusalem and the Great Pyramid had been proposed earlier. The French delegates were particularly outspoken for Paris. Greenwich won, but French maps did not acknowledge it until 1914. In a magnificent and rarely seen hall at the Paris Observatory, I paid homage to the old French longitude marker, a line of 32 copper bars set into the lofty ceiling, aging testimony to what might have been: PMT—Paris mean time.

There were other refinements: U. S. time zones in 1883, global time zones in 1884, daylight saving time as early as 1915—all artifices strengthening time's grip on our lives.

Watches had evolved from portable clocks four centuries earlier. The first ones were suspended from belts or worn around the neck, and later carried in pockets. The mass production of pocket watches in the United States began in the 1860s. By then watches on bracelets already had appeared, but they were worn mostly by women. They didn't become popular for men, who thought them too decorative, until World War I, when soldiers found it hard to reach inside their bulky coats to check the time.

Today watches pour off the assembly lines in unbelievable numbers: more than half a billion a year, with some 300,000 sold daily in the United States alone. This leads to my theory—and I welcome challenge—that more timepieces have been built than all other machines combined.

To see an industry pacesetter, I took a train into the mountains of central Japan to a watch factory operated by the Seiko Group, the world's largest timepiece manufacturer. In a 4.5-acre plant, 1,150 robots, moving like figures in a Charlie Chaplin movie, screwed parts into passing watches. Every two seconds a new movement popped off the assembly line.

I recalled to my host, Seiko guide Hiroshi Tsukahara, an earlier visit to Switzerland's watchmaking district in the Jura

BERNARD G. SILBERSTEIN/PHOTO RESEARCHERS

Big Ben towers over the London skyline.

Mountains. There workmen labor for days by hand over individual mechanical watches.

"The Swiss were slow originally to adjust to the new quartz technology," said Tsukahara. I pointed out that the Swiss are selling quartz watches now—and accruing more revenue than Japan. But Seiko alone produces more watches than all Switzerland.

The secret of Seiko's success is the quartz crystal, which it first marketed in a timepiece in 1969. Powered by battery, a crystal in a quartz watch vibrates 32,768 times a second. An integrated circuit—a series of tiny electric switches—counts the vibrations and converts them to a dial, standard or digital. In the latter there are no moving parts.

"The trick was to make the crystal in the shape of a tiny tuning fork," said Kinji Fujita, who was a member of the team responsible for Seiko's first quartz watch. "This decreased the size of the oscillator and cut power consumption." Today an inexpensive quartz watch runs more accurately than the best mechanical watch made, which is faithful within about a second a day.

In the face of the digital dial's popularity, is the standard watch dial facing extinction? I doubt it. A digital readout does time intervals better. But it gives little relative information, such as how far it is from 5:45 to 6 o'clock. Besides, how will a child of digital time know what "clockwise" means?

Have we become slaves to the clock? David Landes, a historian of timekeeping at Harvard University, thinks not.

"The clock let individuals know what time belonged to their employers and what time was their own. Workers are now actually freer than ever before. Without the clock, and now the watch, there is no modern world. It is the difference between a complex, intricately coordinated society and a primitive one only vaguely aware of time's possibilities."

A vast global timekeeping system keeps all civilization synchronized.

How important this network is I saw for myself one chill November day in China. As I watched with a group of scientists in a frigid observatory near Xian, Ukrainian folk dancers stomped and spun in a television program broadcast from the Soviet Union, relayed by a satellite hovering above Indonesia. "Hmm," said Wu Guei-chen, China's chief timekeeper, "this program is better than most."

Wu and scientists in Shanghai and Beijing tune in Soviet television at 9:59 every evening—not for amusement but to check atomic clocks in the three cities.

By timing the TV signal's arrival, they can tell if one of these clocks is running fast or slow. China's single time zone, stretching 3,000 miles from Shanghai to Tibet, is synchronized by a signal from the observatory where we sat freezing. China's continuing effort to keep time to within a billionth of a second a day began as part of modernization, to join the rest of the industrialized world.

Most of us in or out of China couldn't care less about what time it is to within a billionth of a second. In human terms, even as you watch a second tick away, it's gone.

But our technological world needs the precise time. A navigator at sea or aloft, plotting his location by satellite, relies on a time signal accurate to within a single millionth of a second (microsecond). Deep space probes like the planetary explorer Voyager II are guided by radio signals timed to billionths of a second (nanoseconds).

And physicists tracking motion inside an atomic nucleus reckon in picoseconds (trillionths of a second) or even femtoseconds (thousandths of a picosecond). To grasp this, consider that there are more femtoseconds in one second than there were seconds in the past 31 million years.

David Allan, a time theorist at the National Institute of Standards and Technology, points out that the past does not exist except in our memory. "Nor the future, except in our expectations of it," he says. "The most a clock gives is the time an instant ago—not even the time now."

A clock also says how long something takes. We find this intriguing, I think, because interval time—in sports, science, driving down the interstate, or in the rhythms of music, dance, and poetry—usually involves action.

Zeno of Elea, a fifth-century B.C. Greek, was the first to wonder how a specific interval could consist of smaller intervals that could be subdivided endlessly. The paradox has bewildered the ages.

But Dave Allan doesn't worry much about Zeno. To Allan a second is virtually infinite. "We can split a second into as many pieces as our technology allows. There appears to be no limit. Timekeeping is our own invention."

The clock instructs us when—maybe even how—to behave. Each hour is a little bucket of time to fill. The clock says when to pour.

Nature too has its clocks. We can read them almost everywhere if we have the tools. In 1947 American chemist Willard Libby found a clock ticking in virtually everything that lived during the past 50,000 years—the carbon-14 atom, which decays at a known rate. By comparing carbon-14 atoms with atoms that don't decay, scientists can tell the age of a pharaonic mummy or an ancient Indian hearth.

Using similar techniques, geologists can measure decay rates of radioactive elements like uranium, potassium, or rubidium to set ages for the planet's many tiers of rock. Those at the floor of the Grand Canyon reveal two billion years of geologic history, while rocks in northwest Canada go back nearly four. Moon rocks date back 4.5 billion years, about the same age estimated for the earth.

Astronomers have gazed even further back in time. By looking at light from a faraway galaxy, they are actually looking at the galaxy as it was billions of years ago—today the best way to travel in time. The rate at which these galaxies are flying away from each other tells them the date when all the matter in the universe set out on its journey.

"We were able to show that the matter in the universe must have been infinitely compressed and dense about 15 billion years ago," says theoretical physicist Stephen Hawking of England's Cambridge University.

And before that? "Time as we measure it simply did not exist," said Hawking. The reason is that the other side of the beginning of time is an abiding mystery, an unfathomable darkness without matter or motion. And to modern scientists, motion and time are invariably linked.

For Isaac Newton time had a life of its own—an almost divine process cutting a path across all nature. Einstein changed all that with his theories of relativity. As the experiment with the traveling clocks showed, time for Einstein depends on how fast you're traveling. It no longer is absolute. And events determine how fast time passes instead of the other way around—the way I think most of us would like to view it.

I asked Stephen Hawking, often regarded as this half century's answer to Albert Einstein, to explain relative time.

"There is only one absolute," Hawking told me. "It is not time but the speed of light"—186,282 miles a second. In a sense the speed of light is Einstein's master clock, since there can be no velocity without time and the speed of light never varies. So the speed of light really is the best way to measure a meter.

But there's a hitch.

One thing that affects both light and time is gravity. In the universe of Einstein's relativity, gravity is caused by the intrusion of a large chunk of matter like the sun into space and time. It is a geometric effect, like the one you see if you place a bowling ball on a trampoline.

Gravity bends both space and time. Thus in the presence of a large stellar object, light has to travel farther between two points, and time slows down, relativistically speaking. This does present a problem. On the surface of Jupiter, with 318 times the mass of earth, a cesium clock would run noticeably slower than one at home. And what happens then to our light-measured meter?

John Wheeler, an eminent Princeton physicist and friend of Einstein, likes to take the idea to an extreme. He pictures what happens on the surface of a black hole, a superdense body created when a massive star collapses of its own gravitational pull. A black hole's gravity field is so intense that not even light can escape its surface, and time would stand still there.

"This shows us," says Wheeler, who gave black holes their name, "that time is a measuring tool, not an absolute flow or a substance."

Without an event, there is no time. This means, Wheeler believes, that time may be a secondary feature of nature, not a basic one.

"But we're only talking about the physics of time here," says Wheeler. "As much as anybody else, Einstein recognized that the mind's perception of time is a more subtle matter."

This kind of time—of our bodies and minds—has origins deep in a primordial past long before a set of gears on the wall told us when to go to bed.

The body's dominant time cycle is called the circadian rhythm, from the Latin *circa*, approximately, and *dies*, day. The control mechanism for this body clock is believed to lie in the brain's hypothalamus above the roof of the mouth. For most of us a normal circadian cycle is 25 hours, give or take 15 minutes.

Why not 24?

"Being slightly out of sync with nature may have created a kind of tension necessary for survival," explained Charles Ehret, president of General Chronobionics near Chicago. Fascinating. If the planet ever does go to a 25-hour day, will we lose our edge?

A number of body-clock watchers believe we also tick to an array of weekly cycles. These regulate changes in body chemicals, the response pattern of the immune system, and a cyclic rise and fall of heartbeat and blood circulation. These rhythms, some chronobiologists believe, may help explain the designation of the seven-day week as a unit of time—the only calendar unit that does not trace its origins to astronomy.

Charles Ehret is certain that if you abuse these powerful internal rhythms—circadian or otherwise—you are in for trouble. Afternoon drowsiness, the Monday morning blues, jet lag, even sleep disorders and depression can result from the mismatch between the clock on the wall and the ones in the body.

"The invention of the clock may have freed us from the natural cycles of the heavens," said Ehret. "But it did not free us from the natural cycles within."

The Western idea that past, present, and future are arranged in a straight line—that time does not repeat—seems to have grown out of a Judeo-Christian tradition in which events like the creation and Christ's resur-

A teenager consults his watch, a constant companion, to keep his busy day on schedule.

RICHARD HUTCHINGS/PHOTO RESEARCHERS

rection take on special meaning because they occur in a sequence. It may also lead to a belief in life after death, rather than earthly reincarnation.

Today when we glance at the clock and rush out the door, we are running our lives by a system of Babylonian numerology coupled with Egyptian technology within the framework of an Old Testament creation epic—all synchronized by a technology that can split a second into unlimited pieces.

"Linear time has proved to be a convenient and comfortable way to view time, at least in Europe and North America," said Princeton science historian Michael S. Mahoney. "But more important, it led to the idea of progress, so important to the West."

Efficiency aside, does our concept of time as a one-way track also lie at the heart of the follies of our "you-only-go-around-once" culture? The cult of youth, the type A personality, a relentless consumerism always in search of something new? New Mexico anthropologist Edward T. Hall believes this scheduled, time-ordered, scientific existence is controlled by what he calls "monochronic" time.

In contrast, Hall says, many peoples of Asia, the Middle East, Africa, and South America live in "polychronic" time. Everything goes on at once—talking, eating, reading, praying. Scant heed is paid the clock; schedules are flexible. And nobody minds.

Similarly, almost everybody may have lived this way once, since time was usually viewed as a circle, turning back or in on itself, all things possible at all times. This view of time remains central to Buddhist and Taoist belief, in which linear history is a fiction, since all things return to a former state.

East or West, all of us may see time both ways, depending on the circumstances. Still, the competing metaphors can help explain cultural differences: the hazard of making a one p.m. appointment in Burkina Faso, or the folly of presenting a digital watch to a Buddhist monk on his birthday.

Psychologists say our conscious selves inhabit only a brief moment of the present—a little moving slot of invididivual time six to twelve seconds long that we carry along with us all our lives. The present cannot be instantaneous, or we would not be able to make the connections between words or music or other stimuli that transform them into coherent experiences. Tests show that other creatures lack the ability to make time-separated connections.

Can awareness of time be eliminated altogether? In northern Arizona an old Hopi Indian woman talks of a close friend, dead for several years, as if he just stepped out the door.

"Hopi verbs make no distinction between past and present," explained P. David Seaman, a linguist at Northern Arizona University in Flagstaff. "All time runs together, something like an ever continuing present."

Clocks and calendars create the illusion that we live in a world of mathematically measured segments of time. No timekeeping device symbolizes this illusion more than the most famous mechanical clock ever built.

On a fine summer morning I climbed the tower above London's Houses of Parliament with Brian Davis, who helps keep the great clock working. At the top loomed a weight-driven mechanism of gears and levers spanning 15 feet and paced by a 685-pound pendulum that takes two seconds between tick and tock. The minute hands on the clock's four faces are each 14 feet long and travel 119 miles a year at the tip.

The most famous clock is also one of the loudest. Its chimes carry four miles. We climbed to the belfry where Big Ben resides. There is a story that a 19th-century works commissioner of vast girth inspired the name for the 13½-ton bell. For decades it so symbolized power that the British Broadcasting Corporation broadcast its chimes live on the quarter hour.

There are several versions of a story that two workmen a few years ago griped about their boss just as the microphones were turned on. Their explicit words were carried around the globe. Now the BBC rarely picks up the bells live.

Our scientists can break a second down to a thousandth of a trillionth part. We have an idea when time began and that it may not run forever. Biologists assure us that our body itself is as much a part of the clockwork universe as any clock we ever built. And we know that physical time is relative—that it depends on things that happen instead of the other way around.

But what of the questions we all have about time: Can we travel through it, or can it be reversed? Who has not wished to turn back clock or calendar—to erase mistakes, to return as a child with adult wisdom, to ride with Alexander through Asia or chat with Shakespeare?

Common sense says it's impossible: Look at a film of an egg as it falls to the floor and breaks. Run the film backward. Watch the egg reassemble, then rise through the air.

This demonstrates a basic law of science: that nature is a process of disorganization, not organization. This increasing natural disorder—or entropy—is based on the principle that there are more possible disordered states in nature than there are ordered states.

This tendency toward disorder is called an arrow of time. There is also a psychological arrow of time, which likewise gives us a sense that time is passing in just one direction. It is the reason we remember the past, but not the future. The fact that the universe is expanding and not contracting gives us another arrow of time. All these arrows persuade most scientists that time can move in only one direction.

Yet physicists find it useful to visualize backward-running time at the subatomic level, in the energy-matter exchanges taking place deep in the atom's interior.

"Sometimes when a subatomic particle is converted into energy, it is possible to look at it as if the energy, going backward in time, created the particle," Richard Feynman of Caltech had said. "We don't know that this happens anywhere else."

Three other physicists—Kip S. Thorne, Ulvi Yurtsever, and Michael S. Morris—speculated in a study at Caltech that the laws of physics might not forbid time travel—at least in principle. A subatomic particle by traveling through a "wormhole," a short-cut between two points widely separated in space, might simultaneously tunnel backward in time. However, even if physical law permits such travel, they highly doubt that humans will ever achieve it in practice.

"Time is the best teacher," a philosopher once wrote. "Unfortunately, it kills all its pupils." Today some of the pupils are attempting to outwit the master.

In Oakland, California, clients of a company called Trans Time, Inc., are signing up to have their bodies—or just their heads—frozen when they die. The bodies and heads are stored in stainless-steel capsules filled with liquid nitrogen until some point in the future when death is vanquished and science is able to revive and restore them. Unable to defeat time, they are attempting to arrest a natural process—aging and death.

Today we seem bent on either expanding time by living longer or packing more into ever briefer periods. Our TV ads, for example, are electronically compressed to give more bang for the buck. Many viewers find such ads more vital and convincing. But Jeremy Rifkin, author of *Time Wars: The Primary Conflict in Human History*, deplores this fixation with efficiency and speed. "The humanity is sapped out of the life process because there is no room for experiencing, for savoring, or for just being."

Nevertheless, time is what we make of it. Says Harvard's David Landes: "We could time track events and swimming meets in thousandths or millionths of seconds, but we don't. We ultimately are still in control of how we use time and how it affects us."

But, still, what *is* time?

After all my travels and talking and reading, I believe that Professor Wheeler's concept of time comes the closest to an actual explanation: that it is a dimension and, like any other dimension, only a secondary quality in nature.

But we humans have internalized it so powerfully that time has taken on a meaning all its own. We run our lives by numbers on clocks and calendars that we ourselves have created. We already anticipate Saturday, January 1, 2000. But in the grand scheme of things, it will be just another day.

Here's a rousing, rhythmic poem that will have you tapping your toes and checking your watch. But look out for Daylight Savings Time, or you will also be "back too soon."

Half Past June

By Arnold Spilka

I looked at my watch
Clucked like a hen
Kissed my elbows
And looked again!
Help! I cried
It's half past June
If I don't hurry
I'll be back too soon!
And before I could think
Or knew what I meant
I jumped on my back
And was gone where I went!

What you need to know about this son of a barber is that he invented the water clock, which is not as portable as a Swatch, but served the people of his day well.

Ctesibius

The Egyptian metropolis of Alexandria became one of the great centers of learning, research, and invention in the ancient world. The goal of every scientist, philosopher, and student was to study in Alexandria. Some, like Archimedes, left their native countries to do so. Others, such as Ctesibius, were born there.

Facts about Ctesibius' life are few. The son of a barber, he was born during the third century B.C. and at an early age became known for his mechanical ability and ingenuity. Which inventions are his and what modifications he made to other inventions may never be known for certain, since no original work of his has come down to us. We do know that he was fascinated with the possibilities water offered, and the invention of the water organ and the water clock are both commonly attributed to Ctesibius.

The Water Organ

A player needed to use both his hands and feet to operate Ctesibius' water organ. The diagram included here is a modern reconstruction of Ctesibius' water organ. To create and maintain a steady flow of air, a person pressed the lever arm (H). This action moved the piston (B) upward in the cylinder (A), which in turn forced the air in A to pass through the valve (C) into a globe (D). If B sank down, by its own weight, air was drawn back into A and then again forced into D. The air that accumulated in D pressed down on the water surrounding it, causing the level of the water outside to rise. The pressure of this water made the air in D and the box (E) rush through the organ pipe (G). When a musician struck a key (F), the stopper piece below G was pushed back until a passageway for the air was created from D to G—producing a sound. The length and width of the individual pipes determined the type of sound.

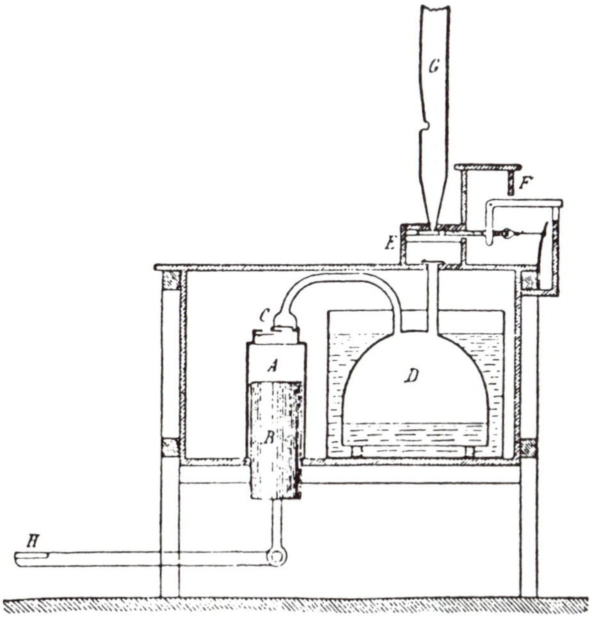

The Water Clock

Knowing the exact time was not as important in ancient times as it has become today. Sundials were commonly used, but they had many drawbacks: They required sun, they gave only approximate time, and they required special positioning in respect to the longitude and latitude of each location.

Water clocks date back to at least 1500 B.C. The ancients used the water clock in the courtroom to limit the time each lawyer could speak. Various sources credit Ctesibius with several improvements in water clock design.

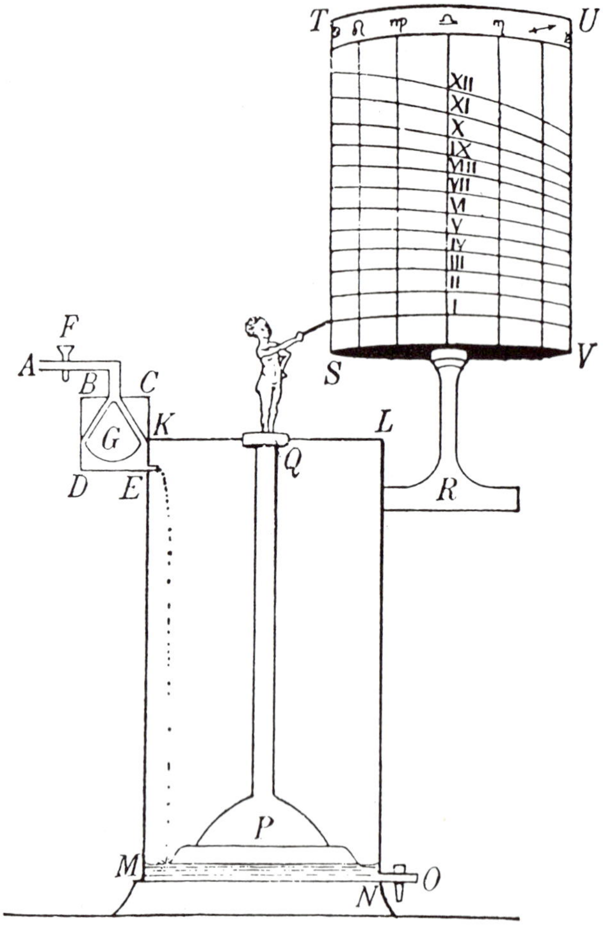

Exactly how the water clock worked is not certain. Ancient texts are not clear about the details. Hermann Diels, an early twentieth-century German scientist, is credited with the best reproduction and explanation of how the water clock developed or enhanced by Ctesibius might have functioned.

Water flowed through A into G. From this holding vessel, the water slowly dripped via the small opening labeled E into a container (KLMN). The mechanism was advanced enough to enable users to control the rate of flow and make it uniform. Therefore, the amount of water collecting in the vessel provided a fairly accurate measure of time. To indicate the amount of time that had passed, a float (P) was attached by a rod to a stand (Q) on which stood a figure with a pointer in his hand. Attached to KLMN is the base (R) of another cylinder (TUSV).

Around the upper rim of the latter are the twelve signs of the zodiac. Along the side of the cylinder is a graduated scale. The ancients divided daytime into twelve hours and nighttime into twelve hours. Hence, the length of the hour varied according to the season—i.e., shorter daytime hours and longer nighttime hours in winter and vice versa in summer. The graduated scale took all this into account. Thus, as the water rose in cylinder KLMN, the pointer indicated the hour on cylinder TUSV. When P had floated to the top, the day was done. O was then unplugged to allow the water to exit, and the process began again.

Time marches on, but the future is always just around the corner. Those who look ahead may be inventing blue jeans for the 21st century today. Act now, it's never too soon.

Futuristic Frocks

What will the well-dressed worker wear in the 21st century? Not pinstripes and not polyester, say student fashion designers.

A recent Suit of the Future contest displayed the visions of fashion students from around the country. One design reflected fears of what the future holds. Kristin Shroeder, prizewinner from Virginia Commonwealth University, used patent leather in her design as a material able to endure radiation and acid rain. Other students created jumpsuits with a built-in mobile communications system and piped-in music.

13

HELPING HANDS WHEN TIME RUNS OUT

China's Troubled Animals

The Chinese government recognizes 47 species of mammals, 44 birds and 6 reptiles as being in special trouble, and these have been given full protection. Even so, hunting, or habitat destruction or both threaten them all. With the rapid disappearance of rain forest in Yunnan province and elsewhere, various mammals, especially treetop primates, are seriously threatened and declining in number. And with the draining of wetlands, alligators and 5 to 8 crane species are now endangered. Sumatran rhino, saiga antelope, Malayan tapir and saltwater crocodile are already extinct in China. This chart lists a sample of China's rare and unique wildlife.—George Schaller

Przewalski's horse **1**

Extinct in the wild since the 1950s. A reintroduction program with zoo-bred animals has been started. More than 20 individuals are in a walled enclosure in Xinjiang. Once the herd reaches 80, some animals will be liberated in their former pasturelands of nothern Xinjiang.

Snow leopard **2**

Partial to rugged terrain, snow leopards are found widely in the mountains on and around the Tibetan Plateau as well as in the Tian Shan, Altai, Kunlun and other mountains of Xinjiang. Everywhere rare, they are shot and trapped for their pelts, their bones (for medicine), and because they may kill livestock. Perhaps as many as 2,000 survive in the country, but numbers everywhere are decreasing.

Argali sheep **3**

Several races occur in China, all decimated through hunting and now rare. Two are of serious concern. Only one population of Marco Polo sheep with about 150 animals survives along the border with Afghanistan and USSR in western Xinjiang. Some of these are protected in the Taxkorgan Reserve. The Tibetan argali was once found all over the Tibetan Plateau, but it is now the rarest wild hoofed animal there, with only small herds in remote places. Argalis still lack full protection in China.

Wild yak **4**

The ancestor of the domestic yak, it is confined to the Tibetan Plateau; except for strays into India, all are in China. Hunted heavily for meat, it has been exterminated over most of its range. Survives mainly in the remote northwestern part of the Plateau. Found in only one reserve—the 17,300-square-mile Arjin Shan Reserve.

Black-necked crane **5**

Breeds only on the Tibetan Plateau. Except for a few in India, all birds nest in China. Nesting marshes are much disturbed by people, domestic animals and dogs. Little hunted on Plateau but may be killed when migrating to low elevations in winter. An estimated 600–1,000 remain.

Tibetan antelope **6**

With its long lyre-shaped horns, this is one of the most beautiful of all antelopes. Found only on the Tibetan Plateau, usually above 14,500 feet, the species prefers flat to rolling terrain. Hunting has eliminated it over much of its range; last stronghold is in the northwestern part of Plateau. Herds migrate widely in search of forage. Number unknown but still in thousands.

Eld's, or brow-antlered, deer **19**

In China, occur only on Hainan Island where about 120 survive, most of them semi-wild in an enclosure. As in other parts of its range from India to Indochina, the species is on the verge of extinction due to hunting and destruction of wetlands and other habitats.

White-headed langur **14**

Discovered only in 1952 in southwestern Guangxi, this rain forest monkey has a restricted distribution of about 200 square miles. Only a few hundred individuals remain. Killed locally for use as a tonic.

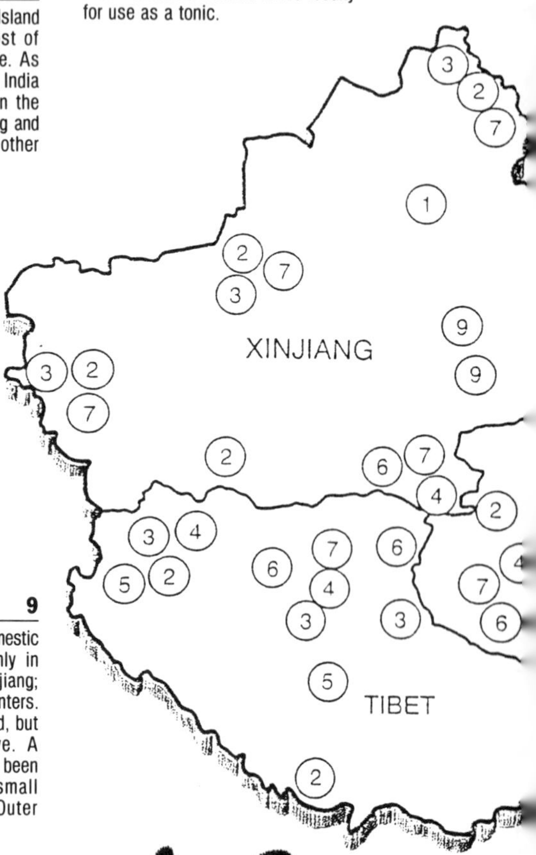

Brown bear **7**

Although once widespread in the forests of Northeast China, and on the alpine pastures of many mountain ranges, it has been relentlessly persecuted for meat, medicine and hides, so much so that it is now gone from much of its range. A distinct race on the Tibetan Plateau is the most seriously threatened mammal there. Brown bears still lack full protection. No estimate of numbers is available.

White-lipped deer **8**

Found in the eastern part of the Tibetan Plateau where it inhabits mountain forests and upland pastures. Number unknown but several thousand of the elk-sized species still occur in scattered populations. Farmed for the medicinal value of its antlers.

Bactrian camel **9**

The ancestral species of the domestic two-humped form. Found mainly in remote deserts of eastern Xinjiang; elsewhere exterminated by hunters. No census has been conducted, but several hundred may survive. A 4,000-square-mile reserve has been established for them. (A small population also occurs in Outer Mongolia.)

Gibbon **10**

Three species of gibbon—crested, white-handed and hoolock—occur in Yunnan. All of these elegant apes are rare, their tropical forest habitat small, fragmented and shrinking. Hoolock gibbon are most threatened, with perhaps only 100-200 remaining. A distinct race of crested gibbon on Hainan Island has only about a dozen survivors.

Snub-nosed, or golden, monkey **11**

The 3 races of snub-nosed monkey are confined to China. Of these, the Guizhou snub-nosed monkey has the most restricted distribution centering around the Fangjingshan Reserve. Numbers may not exceed 500. The Yunnan snub-nosed monkey may be equally scarce. Locals use its brain for medicinal purposes. The Sichuan snub-nosed monkey—which unlike the others has a golden coat—has a range similar to that of giant pandas and is more abundant than the other races.

Elephant **12**

A few herds remain in Yunnan near the borders of Vietnam, Laos and Burma. Fewer than 100 elephants may persist in China.

Giant panda **13**

Found in 3 provinces (Shaanxi, Gansu, Sichuan) the panda inhabits a vestige of its former range which once encompassed much of eastern China, as well as northern Burma and Vietnam. Through hunting and forest destruction, the panda population has become fragmented and now occurs in about 25 isolated habitats surrounded by cultivation. Total range is about 6,000 square miles, number of animals around 1,000; both habitat and numbers are shrinking.

Yangtze River dolphin, or baiji **18**

Threats to this endemic species include pollution, collision with boats and capture by fishermen. The proposed Three-Gorges Dam on the Yangtze would eliminate 125 miles of vital habitat. Perhaps only 200 remain. Attempts will be made to retain a few in a semi-wild state.

Tiger **23**

Five races once roamed China. One race, formerly of Xinjiang, is extinct and all others are still declining in number because of hunting. The South China tiger—unique to the country—once inhabited 14 provinces. From an estimated 4,000 in 1949, it has been reduced to 30-40 today. The Siberian tiger in Northeast China has been reduced to about 30, but about 200 are more or less protected on the USSR side of the border.

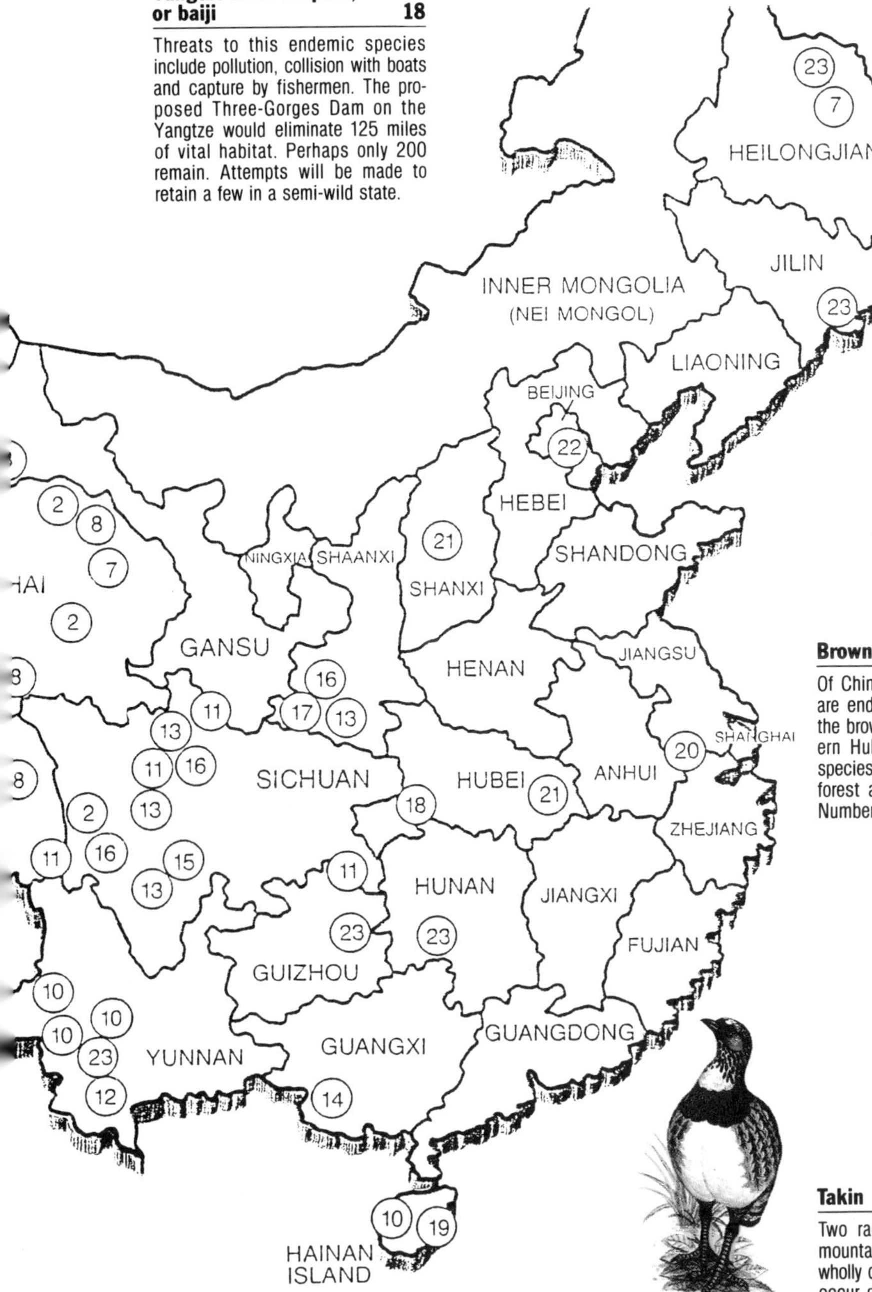

Père David's deer **22**

Extinct in the wild for centuries. Most wetland habitat destroyed. Last captive herd in China—in the imperial hunting park near Beijing—killed in 1900. In 1985, 22 deer returned to the site of the old park from England. That herd now numbers more than 70. A second semi-wild herd has also been established.

Brown eared pheasant **21**

Of China's 25 pheasant species, 11 are endangered, none more so than the brown eared. Found in northeastern Hubei and central Shanxi, the species may be limited to three small forest areas, two of them reserves. Numbers unknown.

Chinese alligator **20**

Once widespread in Yangtze River lowlands. Land reclamation has destroyed most habitat. Fewer than 500 remain in wild.

Takin **16**

Two races of takin—a ponderous mountain relative of musk ox—are wholly confined to China. Golden takin occur only in the Qinling Mountains where several hundred persist. Sichuan takin, more numerous than the golden, share most forests with the giant panda. Habitat destruction threatens their future outside reserves.

Sichuan hill partridge **15**

Endemic to southern Sichuan, this partridge has a restricted distribution of only 3,500 square miles of mountain forests—all of which are being logged. No reserve exists for the species. Number unknown.

Crested ibis **17**

One of the rarest birds in the world. Formerly found widely in Korea, Japan and eastern China. Presumed extinct in the wild until in 1981 seven birds were found in Qinling Mountains near Xian. Given protection, this small colony has increased to more than 40.

Conservationists are trying to protect the endangered black rhino from poachers in the nation of Namibia in Southwest Africa. Its horn, worth up to $18,000 per pound on the black market, is believed to have "magical" medicinal powers, but is also used in dagger handles.

The Black Rhino

Photograph by Anthony Bannister

Martin Britz of Namibia's Nature Conservation Department slices off the horns of an anesthetized black rhino. The painless surgery is part of a bold and controversial plan to keep poachers from slaughtering the vanishing giant for its valuable horn.

14

SIGN OF THE TIMES: FACTOIDS

From the March 1990 Career World *comes news of workers in remote locations. If you're tired of your parents being away on business, you may see the value in having them nearby, and their company HQ* far *away.*

Going On-Line Worldwide

The presence of computers in our daily life is an undisputed fact. Computers have become an accepted member of the work force on the local, national, and international business scene. Due to the increasing sophistication of telephone, computer, and satellite communications, the international use of computers has grown so much that inexpensive overseas workers are increasingly being recruited and trained to perform services—telephone sales, word processing, and computer programming—thousands of miles away from the business's home base.

These workers, dubbed "electronic immigrants," have become a controversial trade and political issue of the 21st century, says futurist Joseph Pelton. Jobs are being exported to foreign workers, leaving a gap in the U.S. job market.

With more and more human commuters working in their homes, a new kind of road is needed for computer commuting. Imagine the days before interstates and freeways, when traveling across country meant winding roads, lots of stops, and slow speeds. It may sound relaxing, but it took forever to get anywhere. *Electronically transmitted information is facing the same kinds of traffic jams.*

Computer 'Superhighway' to Link Nation's Computers

A "superhighway" system may soon link supercomputers at more than 1,000 research centers throughout the United States.

Instead of transporting autos and trucks as our present interstate highway system does, the supercomputer superhighway system will transport information at the rate of 50,000 pages a second. The computer network will be an important step toward the goal of wiring the nation so that people in homes and businesses can send pictures, tap huge electronic libraries, and receive high-quality TV pictures.

Today, a series of networks links many computers at different colleges, universities, and government science labs. However, the system is much slower than the proposed supercomputer network. The fastest part of the present network can transmit only 1.5 million bits of data, or about 50 pages of information, a second.

A faster, expanded computer network is needed, say scientists, because of the increasing use of supercomputers. A supercomputer can compute huge amounts of data at amazingly fast speeds. It is used to help forecast weather, to produce models of new airplanes, and to map genes in cells.

Building the supercomputer network, say scientists, will also enable the United States to maintain its position as the world leader in supercomputing.

In the January 1990 issue of Career World *comes the happy report that fewer and fewer of you will have to leave home in order to report to work. Rejoice!*

There's No Place Like Home

That's the slogan for 14 million members of the work force. They are saying "yes" to working at home and "no" to highway traffic jams, subways, and office interruptions. For 5 million of these homebound folk, employers have agreed to keep them on the payroll, turning them into "telecommuters."

The shrinking cost and size of office equipment has made this switch possible. Prices for personal computers, copiers, and fax machines have dropped, and a home office can be assembled for as little as a few thousand dollars, a minor expense for large companies.

Some big businesses see this as a plus for them, too. Companies like J.C. Penney find they can save on office space and expenses while increasing worker productivity by as much as 25 percent.

Working at home is not for everyone, as some workers have returned to their office saying that they missed the office camaraderie, and breaks at home are few and far between. Space problems affect the home worker as well: One worker said he had to go back to the office because his office outgrew his living room. And being removed from work-force action has forced another home worker to get back to the office—she felt she was losing out to the competition.

You could call this "The Way Things Work" in Hollywood. And once you digest this news, you may notice so many labels in the movies that you start to miss the plots.

Movies that Move Products

Remember the cool Ray-Ban sunglasses Tom Cruise wore in *Risky Business*? Ray-Ban is one of many companies that have paid for their products to appear in movies. You can usually spot from 10 to 15 such products—from soda and jeans to cars and sneakers—in just one movie. Product placements like these are big business. Companies who pay for them hope that if the movie hits, their products will hit, too. Movie producers also benefit from the deals. Fees paid for the spots help cover film production costs. So does anyone lose? Perhaps only moviegoers who don't want to sit through two-hour commercials.

15

CAUSE FOR CELEBRATION

Of course, no one knew that the first Thanksgiving was *the first Thanksgiving; the Pilgrims simply wanted to celebrate their lack of want. James A. Able, Jr., reported in* Cobblestone's *November 1989 issue that Sarah Josepha Hale, the woman who wrote "Mary Had a Little Lamb," suggested to Abraham Lincoln's Secretary of State that the holiday be official. He and Lincoln agreed. That was in 1863, and we've been celebrating ever since.*

Harvest Celebration

By Jeanne Field Olson

Mary Brewster, Ellen Bilington, Elizabeth Hopkins, and Susannah Winslow awakened before dawn on the day the Pilgrims had set aside to celebrate their first successful harvest in the fall of 1621. Roasting wildfowl, baking bread, and boiling vegetables, the four women prepared a feast for the fifty Pilgrims and as many Indians as might accept Governor Bradford's invitation to join them. After months of seemingly endless work, the Pilgrims planned to celebrate with three days of recreation, feasting, and prayer amid the brilliant red and gold leaves of New England.

The Pilgrim men also were busy. Four hunters sent out by Governor Bradford brought back many wild ducks, geese, and turkeys. The men cut wood, built cooking fires, and made rough tables of long wooden planks laid on sawhorses. They carried stools and benches from their houses.

Barefoot boys found time for a lively game of stool-ball between carrying wood and water, digging clams, and gathering nuts for the feast. The girls, wearing long, full-skirted dresses of dark red, green, blue, and other dark colors, helped cook and serve.

The Pilgrims must have been dismayed when Massasoit, leader of the Wampanoags, and ninety braves walked out of the forest. Feeding so many braves could have left the Pilgrims little food for winter, but the Indians killed five deer to contribute to the feast.

Corn bread, and perhaps some "Injun and rye" bread, were baked in the outdoor ovens. (Injun and rye was a dark, heavy bread made of cornmeal and barley or rye.) A bit of old butter, salt meat, and ship's biscuit remaining from the *Mayflower* stores were served. The Pilgrims served no fruit jams or cranberry sauce at their feast, as they had no sugar to make them. Wild cranberries grew in local bogs, but only later would they learn to use them.

The settlers roasted wild turkeys, geese, and ducks and boiled lobsters, clams, and eels. The Indians cooked venison over open campfires. Boiled carrots, turnips, and pumpkin were served, as were leeks, watercress, and other salad herbs.

Though thankful for such strange new American foods as turkey, corn, and pumpkin, the Pilgrims still longed for English beef, wheat bread, and beer. In later years, the Pilgrims drank cider, milk, and a beer

The Mayflower *remained at Plymouth until April 1621, housing people until homes could be built. A scene of its departure for England was engraved for an 1894 calendar.*

they brewed from parsnips, pumpkins, and walnut-tree chips. At this feast in 1621, they drank mostly water.

Dried berries and wild plums were their only dessert. Pumpkin and other American fruit pies were not created until sugar and molasses were obtained from the West Indies. Pies and pumpkin desserts became so important a part of later thanksgiving days that some scoffed at that, calling the feast "St. Pompion's Day." (Pompion was an early name for pumpkin.) One year, a Connecticut town even delayed its thanksgiving celebration until the ship carrying molasses to sweeten the pumpkin pies arrived. In the words of one of America's first folk songs,

> For pottage and puddings and
> custards and pies,
> Our pumpkins and parsnips are
> common supplies.
> We have pumpkin at morning and
> pumpkin at noon,
> If it was not for pumpkin we should
> be undone.

Feasting was only part of the Pilgrims' celebration. The Indians danced and displayed their skill with bow and arrow. The Pilgrims held marksmanship contests for sport and to impress their Indian guests with the power of English muskets.

Pouring black powder down a muzzle and firing a musket in a cloud of smoke and flame made for a dirty business, so the Pilgrim men probably wore their everyday long-sleeved linen shirts with leather or cloth jerkins (jackets) and knee-length leather breeches, long stockings, and shoes or boots.

Those three days were a harvest celebration similar to those the Pilgrims knew in England, but it also was unique in some ways. The Pilgrims set aside that time primarily for recreation to celebrate their survival after a year of doubt and their future in the new land. Puritans did not often allow themselves such time without work, and the Pilgrims did not again celebrate in this way. In later years, however, they often proclaimed a Day of Thanksgiving after gathering their harvest. True Puritan Days of Thanksgiving were days of prayer, which often closed with an evening feast. Though not planned as yearly holidays, a Day of Thanksgiving was proclaimed almost every fall. From that religious tradition and Bradford's record of the 1621 harvest celebration, a myth has grown about America's "First Thanksgiving."

Perhaps it was good that the Pilgrims celebrated their harvest in October or early November. On November 10, 1621, the *Fortune* landed, bringing an additional thirty-five settlers but no supplies. The Pilgrims welcomed the new settlers, but everyone had to go on half rations of food until spring.

After 1621, Days of Thanksgiving were celebrated at irregular intervals, mostly in New England, until President Lincoln proclaimed an annual national Thanksgiving Day in 1863.

Celebrations may be large or small, but it's the spirit that animates the occasion. In this story, a humble house receives a blessing that transforms one night, and perhaps, entire lives.

The Magician

By Uri Shulevitz, adapted from the Yiddish of I. L. Peretz

ONE DAY a magician came to a small village. He was traveling on foot.

"Where from?" the villagers asked.

"Far away," the stranger replied.

"Where to?" they wanted to know.

"The big city," he said.

"Then what are you doing here?" they asked.

"I lost my way," he replied.

He was an odd fellow. He was ragged and tattered, yet he wore a top hat.

He gathered people around him on the street. One minute he was full of tricks, and the next he disappeared. Just like that.

He pulled ribbons out of his mouth and turkeys out of his boots. He whistled, and rolls and loaves of bread danced through the air. He whistled again. Everything vanished!

He scratched his shoe, and there was a flood of gold coins. Yet he looked poor and hungry.

It was the eve of Passover. All the houses in the village were lit up and filled with the smell of festive cooking. And on each table, set for the holiday feast, there stood an extra goblet of wine. It was Elijah's cup, prepared for the prophet, a hoped-for guest in every household on this holiday.

Only one house, where there lived a poor man and his wife, remained dark. They had no food and not even a single candle. Yet they would not ask for help.

"There are people who are worse off than we are," the old man said. "We will manage."

Night came.

"Happy holiday," the old man said to his wife.

"Happy holiday," she replied. But she could not help adding, "Passover is here, and we still have nothing."

"The Maker of the Universe does not abandon his creatures," the old man said. "And if God does not want us to have our own Passover feast, then we must bow to his will and attend someone else's. Come, we'll be welcome at our neighbor's."

At that moment the door opened, and a voice said, "May I be your guest for Passover?"

"I'm sorry," the old man said. "We are poor and have nothing to offer you."

"I have everything we need," the voice replied. The visitor waved his hands, and two lighted candlesticks appeared.

The old couple recognized the magician.

He signaled again, and a beautiful cloth spread itself over the table, which slid quietly to the center of the room. The candlesticks floated slowly down to meet it and settled into place.

"Now we need chairs to sit on!" the magician called out. The wooden benches that had been standing against the walls skimmed the floor and stopped at the table.

"Get soft," he ordered, and the benches became armchairs with pillows as backrests.

Out of nowhere, one object after another, everything that was needed to celebrate the holiday appeared on the table.

The old couple could not believe what they saw.

"There is good magic and evil magic," the old man whispered to his wife. "We must not touch anything. We must be sure that evil is not at work here to tempt and deceive us. Let us go and ask the rabbi's advice." The old

woman threw her shawl over her head, and they hurried to the rabbi's house.

When the rabbi heard their story, he said, "Evil magic cannot create real things. It can only fool the eyes. If you can taste the food and pour the wine, if you can sit in the chairs, then they are real and sent from heaven."

The old couple returned home and found everything just as they had left it. But the magician was gone.

They tasted the food. They poured the wine into glasses. They sat in the armchairs among the soft pillows. Everything was real.

Only then did they know it was not a magician but the prophet Elijah himself who had visited them.

For the really big parties, no one can resist fireworks; and who can sit still when those start booming and sizzling overhead—it's been that way for centuries. But those dazzling displays take planning and attention. Omar Lerman, whose company helped produce the fireworks show at the Statue of Liberty's Centennial celebration in 1986, knows how to light up the skies.

A Short History of Fireworks

By Omar K. Lerman

Thud. Swoosh. And then a line of sparks flying five hundred to a thousand feet into the air. The anticipation is almost as exciting as the event to come. And then it happens. First a flash, then the report. And now a shower of stars streaming across the sky. Finally comes the shock wave and the odor of gunpowder. All this is part of the joy and excitement of fireworks.

Fireworks have been with us for eleven centuries. According to Alan St. H. Brock, a well-known historian of fireworks, the people of China and/or India were the first to discover that three common substances, when mixed together in the proper proportions, would burn with a brilliant and intense light. Some authorities refuse to credit anyone with the discovery, since fireworks spring from fire. Everybody used fire in prehistoric times, and the basic elements for creating fireworks were and still are commonly found. However, it does seem certain that it was the Chinese who organized the information and techniques for making fireworks into a body of common knowledge. When that happened, no one can be certain. Most likely it occurred about eleven hundred years ago.

The most frequent uses of fireworks were almost always related to a ceremony or celebration: weddings, coronations, the change of seasons, births, and just for sheer enjoyment. Before the Chinese used these pleasure-making formulas for destructive purposes, they used rockets, fire lances, and fireballs dropped from walls and flung through the air to alarm people. The next step was the invention of the gun, and around the thirteenth century the principle of using pyrotechnics to propel a missile through a tube closed at one end was perfected.

In the beginning, the effects were simple. The colors produced were variations of flame colors—reds, oranges, and yellows—and the most common form was the firecracker, sometimes used in strings of thousands of individual units. Even today, the Chinese use these "celebration crackers" on their New Year's Day. As the craft was advanced in Asia, the self-propelling rocket and the hand-held sparkler were developed.

Fireworks began to be seen in Europe in the thirteenth century, most likely brought from the Orient by traders. It did not take long for people in the West to master the art, as the formulas and techniques for manufacturing fireworks were extremely simple. In short order, the French, Italians, English, Germans, Russians, and Spanish were making elaborate displays and developing distinctive styles.

The Italians and French favored ground displays, such as fireworks attached to replicas of buildings that were sometimes real, sometimes fanciful. Some of the displays covered acres of land and lasted for hours. The Germans and English concentrated more on the fireworks themselves. Fountains and aerial shells were the most popular pieces in those countries.

Everywhere, the colors were limited and rather murky. It took pyrotechnicians another hundred years to learn how to produce true red, green, silver, and gold. Rich purple and true blue were not perfected until the twentieth century.

By the seventeenth century, fireworks flourished throughout Europe. People went to fireworks displays as they now go to the theater or movies. Great composers wrote music to accompany the displays, and pyrotechnicians were considered to be great artists. By the beginning of the eighteenth century, fireworks were common in the American colonies. Samuel Adams, a signer of the Declaration of Independence, predicted that the Fourth of July would always be celebrated with picnics, parades, and fireworks.

While there have been a number of refinements in the art of pyrotechnics over the past two centuries, the most important advance has been in the method of firing. Until twenty years ago, all fireworks were hand-fired one at a time. A shell was placed in a steel pipe or mortar, and the fuse was lit by a torch. This meant that shells could be fired only as quickly as the mortars could be reloaded, and elaborate shows required teams of people working together.

Today the standard practice is to fire shows electrically. The fuses of each shell are ignited by sending an electrical charge to the shell. Each shell also has a separate mortar, which is never reloaded. With this method, shells can be fired with greater speed in a planned sequence to produce a specific pattern. This technique is similar to designing dance patterns and is referred to by the same name: choreography. Just as in dance, the choreography is done to music.

Twentieth-century masters of the art of pyrotechnics produce shows as magnificent, if not as elaborate, as those of the seventeenth century. The shells fly higher, the combinations of effects are greater, and the colors are richer and more varied. Today fireworks continue to be a popular and exciting form of entertainment.

16

A CELEBRATION OF CHILDREN

You can see here the varied ways in which people of other cultures and other eras have viewed their children. Some look "stylized" to a modern eye—molded and altered until they no longer resemble "real" people. Nevertheless, images of children tell us not only about them, but about the times in which they lived and played.

Children in Art

By Marjorie Jackson

Tutankhamen Hunting, 1360? B.C.

Hunting scenes were popular with artists in ancient Egypt. The hunter driving this racing chariot is Tutankhamen, the boy who became Pharaoh of Egypt when he was only nine. He is famous today as "King Tut," the only Pharaoh whose tomb was found intact, undisturbed by robbers. Among the many treasures archeologists discovered in the tomb was a small chest with this painting on one side. The young Pharaoh shoots at birds and beasts stampeding over dotted sand. Above the horse's plumed headpiece are rows of hieroglyphics.

Portrait of an Etruscan Boy,
early 200s B.C.

This bronze sculpture, originally part of a standing figure, shows an Etruscan boy whose name we don't know. The artist made a clay model of the boy's face to capture his thoughtful expression, because a true likeness was important in Etruscan art. A mold was then made from the clay model, and hot liquid bronze was poured into the mold to make this lasting portrait.

The Crossing of the Red Sea,
A.D. 1181

Nicholas of Verdun, a French artist, sometimes told stories in his works. He made this enamel plaque for a church altar. It shows the Hebrew prophet Moses helping his people to escape from slavery in Egypt. Nicholas used thick and thin curving lines to convey the movement of the figures, rushing with their children and even a pet dog to cross the Red Sea to freedom.

Prince Shōtoku as the Buddhist Saint Jizō, late 1300s

Shōtoku was a highly revered boy-prince in Japan about 700 years ago. An artist at the court painted this portrait of him. Instead of wearing the silks of a ruler, Shōtoku is dressed in coarse robes and straw sandals like a religious pilgrim. He sits on a rocky ledge, as if he were resting during a long walk to a mountain temple. His left hand holds prayer beads, and in his right is the staff of Jizō, a Buddhist saint who is the protector of children.

Self-portrait, 1484

Many artists have painted or sketched portraits of themselves. The German artist Albrecht Dürer drew this self-portrait when he was only thirteen. He said it was very hard to get the eyes just right, because he had to look sideways to see himself in a mirror. He used shading to give his image a natural, rounded look.

Children's Games, 1560

Peasants were the favorite subject of Pieter Breughel the Elder of the Netherlands. He liked to dress in peasant clothes and visit village fairs and weddings, or just sit and do quick pencil sketches of people working or playing. When he had collected enough images to fill a canvas, Breughel would paint the active figures, bringing them to life in brilliant colors. How many of the children's games in this painting do you recognize?

The Maids of Honor, **1656**

Diego Velázquez, a great artist at the Spanish court, was a master at using light in paintings. Here, he spotlighted little Princess Margarita, posing among her maids and playmates. She has just turned, it seems, to look toward the viewer. Has someone called to her? Look at the mirror on the back wall for the answer. The two faces reflected there are her parents, the king and queen, who have entered the hall. Velázquez liked to add this kind of surprise to his paintings. Another surprise here is Velázquez himself, on the left, standing at work before a large canvas.

A Sunday Afternoon on the Island of La Grande Jatte, **1884–86**

The French artist Georges Seurat liked to sketch people strolling in a riverside park. He arranged them like cutouts, frozen in place, and painted them by dotting points of color onto the canvas, trusting the viewer's eye to blend the dots into different shades. Standing in bright sunlight, a small girl in a white dress draws the eye into the picture.

The New School, **c. 1923**

Enormous frescoes by Diego Rivera, a Mexican mural artist, appear on important public buildings throughout Mexico City. Many of Rivera's paintings record scenes from Mexico's history, particularly the struggle of the people during the revolution of 1910. Here, a revolutionary, holding his gun ready, protects a circle of children being taught to read in an open-air school.

The Family, **1937**

The modern painter Joan Miró, born in Spain, said that childhood memories prompted many of his paintings. Miró used bold colors and simple, abstract shapes to create this playful, humorous view of a family.

Hurray for Yani, who, while still in her youth, makes the rest of us look like slug-a-beds—when she was very young, museums put her famous monkeys in their galleries. And, unlike many museum works, her paintings will make you smile.

Yani

By Deborah Churchman
Photo by Chick Harrity

One day when Yani was two and a half years old, her father took her to the zoo near her home in China. Yani was *so* excited when she saw the monkeys. She even wanted to play in the monkeys' cage!

Then she went home and painted circles with a brush dipped in ink. She said they were monkeys. But they looked like circles.

Yani worked and worked on her monkeys, the way some kids work on learning about dinosaurs or playing computer games. Finally, at the age of four, she was able to make incredible monkeys—furry monkeys, playful monkeys, naughty monkeys. Almost everyone who saw Yani's

At a museum in Washington, D.C., Yani points out a detail in a painting she just made. Asked how she was able to paint with lots of people staring at her, Yani said, "I ignored them." Yani woke up from an amazing dream about egrets when she was 11 years old. Then she painted 29 egrets, each one seeming to move on paper. Now age 15, Yani still lives in a little town in China with her parents and brother. She's never had an art lesson. But her paintings have touched people all around the world.

monkeys thought they were wonderful. People from a museum liked her paintings so much that they put on a special show.

By the time Yani was six, she'd made 4000 paintings. And most of them were of monkeys! As she painted, Yani told stories about the monkeys. For example, she'd say the monkeys were hungry, and she'd paint fruit for them to eat.

Now Yani is 15. Her paintings have been shown in China, Japan, Europe, and the United States. Recently they were shown in Washington, D.C.; Kansas City, Missouri; and San Francisco, California.

Yani was born with a special talent and a good imagination. But it was because of seeing those zoo monkeys that she started to use her talents. Yani had wanted to learn how to let them "play" on paper. And that's what she did.

Garden Silhouette. Illustration by Pam Levy

Jack Prelutsky celebrates children in many of his poems, and so does Sesame Street *magazine, where this poem from* The Random House Book of Poetry *recently appeared.*

Children, Children Everywhere

By Jack Prelutsky, from The Random House Book of Poetry *(1983, Random House)*

Children, children everywhere,
children dark and children fair,
children of all shapes and sizes,
children springing odd surprises,
children chasing, running races,
children laughing, making faces,
children cooking mud for dinner,
children, every one a winner.

Children jumping, children wiggling,
children grumping, children giggling,
children singing, sneezing, weeping,
children sometimes even sleeping,
children giving children hugs,
children chewing worms and bugs,
children in their parents' hair,
children, children everywhere.

Some people never outgrow their love for dolls; the lucky Japanese may indulge themselves once a year in a beloved celebration. A famous film-maker, Akira Kurosawa, paid tribute to this festival in his movie Dreams*; here, Elinor Tripato Massoglia explains its origins and symbols.*

Hinamatsuri, The Japanese Festival of Dolls

By Elinor Tripato Massoglia

The Festival of Dolls takes place each year on March third. It has been an important part of Japanese family life for hundreds of years.

About two weeks before the event, mothers set up a stand that looks like a flight of steps. It is covered with red material.

Fifteen dolls are arranged in their own places on the stand. The emperor and empress are put on the top shelf with a gold-colored screen behind them. A container of flowers is placed between them, and a lamp at their side.

The second shelf has a set of three ladies-in-waiting dolls. The third has five musicians. The remaining shelves hold dolls that are ministers, footmen, and servants. Sometimes extra shelves have tiny furniture, dishes, and other things used in a Japanese home.

The dolls on the stand are only for show. Many girls put their favorite play-dolls in other places around the room.

On festival day, friends and relatives visit the girls. The day is spent feasting on "doll cakes" made in the forms of fish, shell-

fish, and vegetables. A holiday drink is served, too.

As the food is eaten, stories are told and games are played. Everyone has a good time. Some stories are about the dolls themselves: how old they are, where they came from, and which special happening or people are connected with them.

When the holiday is over, the dolls are carefully placed in boxes and put away until the next year. No one knows for sure when or how the festival started. But everyone knows that it is one of the ways that Japanese people show their love for their children, their joy and pride in them, and their wish to please them.

Many dolls can be found in the works of this famous author; she was inspired by the toys of her childhood. Perhaps you have favorite playthings that offer clues to your future. Around you may be the seeds of your own success.

Rumer Godden's Dolls

By Eleanor Cameron

When Rumer Godden was four, she received a tiny doll in a matchbox. For Ms. Godden this doll seemed much like herself—every time she was laid down, or defeated, she sprang up again. So it's not surprising that Ms. Godden has written so many stories about dolls: *The Story of Holly and Ivy*, *The Fairy Doll*, *Impunity Jane*, *The Dolls' House*, *Miss Happiness and Miss Flower*, and *Little Plum* (all published by Viking Penguin).

In *Miss Happiness and Miss Flower*, Ms. Godden writes about Japanese dolls. She remembers what it was like to be a small girl far away from her home in India. Nona is lonely and miserable in the middle of a cold London winter, but then two little Japanese dolls are sent to her family. They seem as much out of place and homesick as she is, and so Nona finds out how to make a Japanese home for them. At the back of the book are diagrams and directions for making a Japanese dollhouse.

Rumer Godden's other famous doll book is about Tottie and the Plantaganet family. They live in a drafty old shoe box, but they long for a real home, and so Tottie tells the dolls to *wish*—wish with all their might, because that is the only way dolls can get things done. The dolls' house becomes a reality, but will the beautiful and spiteful Marchpane, a doll made out of stuffed kid, ruin their dreams? Find out in *The Dolls' House*.

17

WHAT'S AN UMBRELLA?

It's big enough to be a parachute—small enough to tuck into a book bag. Dormice and elves have been known to huddle under mushrooms, wishing umbrellas came cut to their size. Umbrellas can be tailor-made, and custom-sized, and plenty of wonderful things have been found beneath their rims: Christopher Robin marching around and saying, "Tut-tut, it looks like rain"; Roman citizens seeking "a shady place"; Mary Poppins, looking for Jane and Michael Banks; two friends walking on a rainy day, safe and dry.

Calling All Brollies

By Kim Conrad

One rainy afternoon in old London town Mr. Jonas Hanway did a brave thing. He buttoned his coat, picked up his green silk umbrella, and went out for a walk.

He hadn't gone very far before it started: rude noises made behind his back, passersby turning to stare. A rock or two skittered past his ankles. You see, that day in 1740 Jonas Hanway's neighbors didn't know what to make of the strange contraption he was carrying. They had never seen such a thing. Some even thought it was an odd sort of musical instrument.

Although umbrellas were new to the English in 1740, they had been around for more than two thousand years. In ancient Egypt the umbrella was used as a sun shade and became a symbol of high rank.

The word *umbrella* comes from the Romans. They called it *umbracala*, which means "shady place." The English, however, found the umbrella more useful for protection from the frequent rain of their country. Once they got used to the umbrella, they gave it all sorts of nicknames, like gamp, bumbershoot, and brolly.

Umbrellas have been used for more than just keeping off sun or rain. In India royal visitors are often welcomed under umbrellas made of silk and decorated with gold and jewels, or feathers. In Japan umbrella-making is such an art that some craftsmen can carve an entire umbrella frame from a single stick of wood.

The world's first parachute was a giant umbrella, fifteen feet wide. It had ribs of whalebone and an eleven-foot handle made of copper. The parachute floated safely for more than nine thousand feet!

Over the years many superstitions have grown up about umbrellas. "Don't hold your umbrella straight up," some said to the early users. "The heat of the sun will be drawn right into your brain!"

"Don't stand under an open umbrella in the house," others warned. "And don't lay it on the bed. It's bad luck."

In one way umbrellas really *are* unlucky. "If you want it to rain," people often joke, "just leave your umbrella at home." And they are always getting lost. In just one year seventy thousand brollies were found on the trains and buses of London.

Fancy umbrellas have been made with writing pens hidden in their handles. There have been bumbershoots that whistle, others with windows. And at a London clothing store, you can buy an umbrella that is exactly your size. Each brolly is cut to fit, like a fine pair of trousers.

Whether your umbrella is plain or fancy, large or small, it deserves a little loving care. When you step inside after a rainstorm, shake off the extra water by opening and closing the umbrella several times. Leave it open to dry so the ribs won't rust.

And the next time you go out in the rain, be on the lookout for some famous umbrella-lovers, like Mary Poppins, Christopher Robin and Pooh, even the girl from the salt carton. You might just see them, under cover!

DIRECTORY OF MAGAZINES

Boys' Life
P. O. Box 152079
1325 West Walnut Hill Lane
Irving, TX 75015-2079

Calliope (formerly *Classical Calliope*)
30 Grove Street
Peterborough, NH 03458

Career World
Field Publications
4343 Equity Drive
Columbus, OH 43228

Children's Digest
P.O. Box 7134
Red Oak, IA 51591-0134

Children's Playmate
P.O. Box 7134
Red Oak, IA 51591-0134

Cobblestone: The History Magazine for Young People
30 Grove Street
Peterborough, NH 03458

Cricket
P.O. Box 2886
Boulder, CO 80322-2961

Current Events
Field Publications
4343 Equity Drive
Columbus, OH 43228

Current Health
Field Publications
4343 Equity Drive
Columbus, OH 43228

Current Science
Field Publications
4343 Equity Drive
Columbus, OH 43228

Faces: The Magazine About People
30 Grove Street
Peterborough, NH 03458

Highlights for Children
Department CA
P. O. Box 269
Columbus, OH 43272-0269

Humpty Dumpty's Magazine
P.O. Box 7134
Red Oak, IA 51591-0134

International Wildlife
Membership Services
National Wildlife Federation
8925 Leesburg Pike
Vienna, VA 22184

Junior Scholastic
P. O. Box 644
Lyndhurst, NJ 07071-9985

National Geographic
National Geographic Society
Washington, DC 20036

National Wildlife
Membership Services
National Wildlife Federation
8925 Leesburg Pike
Vienna, VA 22184

PLAYS: The Drama Magazine for Young People
120 Boylston Street
Boston, MA 02116

Ranger Rick
c/o Ranger Rick's Nature Club
8925 Leesburg Pike
Vienna, VA 22184-0001

Scholastic Choices
Scholastic, Inc.
2931 East McCarty Street
P. O. Box 3710
Jefferson City, MO 65102-3710

Scienceland
Suite 2108
501 Fifth Avenue
New York, NY 10017-6165

Sesame Street Magazine
P.O. Box 55518
Boulder, CO 80322-5518

Sports Illustrated for Kids
P.O. Box 830606
Birmingham, AL 35282-9847

*U*S*Kids*
P.O. Box 8957
Boulder, CO 80322

SUBJECT INDEX

Potter used as a design for a Christmas card, based on the frontispiece from *The Tale of Peter Rabbit*, copyright ©Frederick Warne & Co., 1955; Illustrations: lizard p. 12, by Beatrix Potter, copyright © Frederick Warne & Co., 1955; side view of bat with folded wings p. 13, by Beatrix Potter, copyright © Frederick Warne & Co., 1987; study of a rabbit p. 13, by Beatrix Potter, copyright © Frederick Warne & Co., 1987; side view of a fish p. 14, by Beatrix Potter, copyright © Frederick Warne & Co., 1955; *Amanita muscaria* (fly agaric) with polypody fern and lichen p. 14, by Beatrix Potter, copyright © Frederick Warne & Co., 1987; all reproduced by permission of Penguin Books Ltd., England.

"Ready . . . Set . . . Go!" and the accompanying diagrams appeared in the May 1990 issue of *Boys' Life* magazine, P. O. Box 152079, 1325 West Walnut Hill Lane, Irving, TX 75015–2079; reprinted by permission of *Boys' Life*. Copyright © 1990 *Boys' Life*.

"Start Early, Keep at It, to Learn Map Reading" from the May 1990 issue of *National Geographic* magazine. Reprinted by permission. Copyright © 1990 by the National Geographic Society.

"How a Rabbit Runs" from *Scienceland*, May 1990, Vol. 13 No. 107; reprinted by permission. Copyright © 1990 by *Scienceland*.

The "Try Snowshoeing" artwork appeared in the December 1989 issue of *Boys' Life* magazine, P. O. Box 152079, 1325 West Walnut Hill Lane, Irving, TX 75015–2079; reprinted by permission of the artist. Copyright © 1989 by Steve Chalker.

"'Red Sky at Night; Sailor's Delight'" from *Current Science*, March 30, 1990. Special permission granted by *Current Science* Magazine published by Field Publications. Copyright © 1990 by Field Publications.

The "Hiking Owls" artwork first appeared in the June 1990 issue of *Ranger Rick* magazine, published by the National Wildlife Federation and reprinted by permission. Copyright © 1990 by Lynn Munsinger.

"A Nation of Symbols" from the December–January 1990 issue of *National Wildlife*. Reprinted by permission. Text copyright © 1990 by the National Wildlife Federation. Illustration reprinted by permission of the artist. Copyright © 1990 by Bill Mayer.

"Sacred Trees and Magical Forests" from *Faces*'s September 1989 issue: People of the Forest © 1989, Cobblestone Publishing Inc., Peterborough, NH 03458. Reprinted by permission of the publisher.

"Beliefs About Birds" from *Faces*'s May 1990 issue: Wonderful Birds © 1990, Cobblestone Publishing Inc., Peterborough, NH 03458. Reprinted by permission of the publisher.

"The Firebird" from *Faces*'s May 1990 issue: Wonderful Birds © 1990, Cobblestone Publishing Inc., Peterborough, NH 03458. Reprinted by permission of the publisher.

"Helpful Trees" from *Faces*'s September 1989 issue. Reprinted by permission of the author. Copyright © 1989 by E. Barrie Kavasch.

"All About Mistletoe" from the December 1989 *Children's Playmate*, copyright © 1989 by Children's Better Health Institute, Benjamin Franklin Literary & Medical Society, Indianapolis, Indiana. Used by permission.

"Take Two Leeches and Call Me in the Morning" appeared in the October 1989 issue of *Boys' Life* magazine, P. O. Box 152079, 1325 West Walnut Hill Lane, Irving, TX 75015–2079; reprinted by permission of the author. Copyright © 1989 by D. M. Souza.

"Totem Pole Boy" from the January 1990 issue of *U. S. Kids*. Special permission granted by *U. S. Kids* Magazine published by Field Publications. Copyright © 1990 by Field Publications. Illustration by Mike DiGiorgio.

"Let's Plant a Tree" from the April 1990 issue of *PLAYS*; reprinted by permission of the publisher. Copyright ©1990 by Plays, Inc.

"Alchemy: Golden Heart of the Matter" from *Faces*'s December 1989 issue: The Glory of Gold © 1989, Cobblestone Publishing Inc., Peterborough, NH 03458. Reprinted by permission of the publisher. Engraving, "The Alchemist" courtesy of The Metropolitan Museum of Art, Harris Brisbane Dick Fund, 1926.

"America's First Industry" from *Cobblestone*'s June 1990 issue: Colonial Craftsmen © 1990, Cobblestone Publishing Inc., Peterborough, NH 03458. Reprinted by permission of the publisher. Illustration from *A Tryal of Glasse—The Story of Glassmaking at Jamestown*, published by Eastern National Park and Monument Association.

"Papyrus and Parchment" from *Classical Calliope*'s September 1989 issue: Ancient Inventions © 1989, Cobblestone Publishing Inc., Peterborough, NH 03458. Reprinted by permission of the publisher.

"What the Ancients Used" from *Classical Calliope*'s September 1989 issue: Ancient Inventions © 1989, Cobblestone Publishing Inc., Peterborough, NH 03458. Reprinted by permission of the publisher.

"Housewifely Crafts" from *Cobblestone*'s June 1990 issue: Colonial Craftsmen © 1990, Cobblestone Publishing Inc., Peterborough, NH 03458. Reprinted by permission of the publisher. Illustration from the Alexander Anderson Scrapbook, vol. 1, p. 69; Print Collection, Miriam & Ira D. Wallach Division of Art, Prints and Photographs; The New York Public Library; Astor, Lenox and Tilden Foundations.

"Strawberry Pink Yarn" first appeared in *Cricket* magazine in December 1989. Reprinted by permission of the author. Copyright © 1989 by Theo Elizabeth Gilchrist.

"The Apprentice System" from *Cobblestone*'s June 1990 issue: Colonial Craftsmen © 1990, Cobblestone Publishing Inc., Peterborough, NH 03458. Reprinted by permission of the publisher.

"Falconry" from *Faces*'s May 1990 issue: Wonderful Birds © 1990, Cobblestone Publishing Inc., Peterborough, NH 03458. Reprinted by permission of the publisher. Illustration, Aelbert Cuyp's "Portrait of a Boy with a Falcon," courtesy of The Metropolitan Museum of Art, Purchase, George T. Delacorte, Jr. Gift, 1957.

"Do You See Yourself as a Leader?" from *Career World*, May 1990. Special permission granted by *Career World* Magazine published by Field Publications. Copyright © 1990 by Field Publications.

"Tools of Political Rebellion" from *Cobblestone*'s June 1990 issue: Colonial Craftsmen © 1990, Cobblestone Publishing Inc., Peterborough, NH 03458. Reprinted by permission of the publisher.

"Judith: The Life of a Slave" from *Cobblestone*'s February 1990 issue: The People of Williamsburg © 1990, Cobblestone Publishing Inc., Peterborough, NH 03458. Reprinted by permission of the publisher. Photograph courtesy of the Colonial Williamsburg Foundation, Williamsburg, Virginia.

"The Good Luck Stork" first appeared in the June 1990 issue of *Ranger Rick* magazine, published by the National Wildlife Federation and reprinted by permission. Text copyright © 1990 by Lillian Bason.

"The Kibosh" by Sarah Ellis first appeared in *Cricket* magazine in November 1989. Reprinted by permission of the author. Copyright © 1989 by Sarah Ellis.

"The Silver Dollar" from the November 1989 *Children's Digest*, copyright © 1989 by Children's Better Health Institute, Benjamin Franklin Literary & Medical Society, Indianapolis, Indiana. Used by permission.

"Ugly Ducks Run Amok in Florida Towns" from the September–October 1989 issue of *International Wildlife*. Reprinted by permission. Copyright © 1989 by the National Wildlife Federation.

"Starlings Are No Darlings" from the April–May 1990 issue of *National Wildlife*. Reprinted by permission. Copyright © 1990 by the National Wildlife Federation. Illustration reprinted by permission of the artist. Copyright © 1990 by Jeff Seaver.

"Building Heaven on Earth: America's Utopian Communities" by Naomi Segal. *Junior Scholastic* Magazine, January 12, 1990. Reprinted by permission of Scholastic, Inc., NY.

The "Framed Garden" photograph from the November 1989 issue of *National Geographic* magazine. Reprinted by permission of the photographer. Copyright © 1989 by Michael S. Yamashita.

"Mr. Runkle's Pumpkin" first appeared in *Cricket* magazine in October 1989. Reprinted by permission of the author. Copyright © 1989 by Betse Brydon.

The "Busy Elves" artwork by John O'Brien from the February 1990 issue of *Highlights for Children*. Copyright © 1990 by Highlights for Children, Columbus, Ohio.

"Growing Up in East Harlem" from the May 1990 issue of *National Geographic* magazine. Excerpted by permission of the author. Copyright © 1990 by Jere Van Dyk.

"Ladybug's Garden" first appeared in *Cricket* magazine in May 1990. Reprinted by permission of the author. Copyright © 1990 by Ethel Pochocki. Illustration reprinted by permission of the artist. Copyright © 1990 by Irene Haas.

"A Haunted House" by Charles F. Baker and Rosalie Baker first appeared in *Cricket* magazine, in October 1989. Reprinted by permission of the authors. Copyright © 1989 by Charles F. Baker and Rosalie Baker.

"Empire State Building Camp-Out a Hit" and the accompanying photograph appeared in the September 1989 issue of *Boys' Life* magazine, P. O. Box 152079, 1325 West Walnut Hill Lane, Irving, TX 75015–2079; reprinted by permission of *Boys' Life*. Copyright © 1989 *Boys' Life*.

"Tidying the World's Highest Trash Pit" from the October 1989 issue of *National Geographic* magazine. Reprinted by permission. Copyright © 1989 by the National Geographic Society.

"Take a Skunk to Camp" and the accompanying photo by George Olson appeared in the November 1989 issue of *Boys' Life* magazine, P. O. Box 152079, 1325 West Walnut Hill Lane, Irving, TX 75015–2079; reprinted by permission of *Boys' Life*. Copyright © 1989 by *Boys' Life*.

"Earthquake! Hurricane! Scouts on Both Coasts Aid Survivors" appeared in the March 1990 issue of *Boys' Life* magazine, P. O. Box 152079, 1325 West Walnut Hill Lane, Irving, TX 75015–2079; reprinted by permission of the author. Copyright © 1990 by Sam Chu Lin.

"Counting Noses" appeared in the July 1990 issue of *Boys' Life* magazine, P. O. Box 152079, 1325 West Walnut Hill Lane, Irving, TX 75015–2079; reprinted by permission of the author. Copyright © 1990 by Robert Bahr. Illustration reprinted by permission of the artist. Copyright © 1990 by John Huehnergarth.

"A Fishy Story" from *Current Events*, November 17, 1989. Special permission granted by *Current Events* Magazine published by Field Publications. Copyright © 1989 by Field Publications. Illustration by John Gibson.

"Little Green Riding Hood" reprinted in *Cricket* magazine in July 1990; illustrations reprinted by permission of the artist. Copyright © by Walter Lorraine.

"Championship Whoppers from the Liars Club" appeared in the September 1989 issue of *Boys' Life* magazine, P. O. Box 152079, 1325 West Walnut Hill Lane, Irving, TX 75015–2079; reprinted by permission of the author. Copyright © 1989 by Nino Lo Bello. Illustration reprinted by permission of the artist. Copyright © 1989 by John Huehnergarth.

"Norman Rockwell: Twentieth-Century Storyteller" from *Cobblestone*'s December 1989 issue: Norman Rockwell © 1989, Cobblestone Publishing Inc., Peterborough, NH 03458. Reprinted by permission of the publisher. Illustration, "Triple Self-Portrait," printed by permission of the Norman Rockwell Family Trust. Copyright © 1960 the Norman Rockwell Family Trust.

"April Fool's Fun" from *Cobblestone*'s December 1989 issue: Norman Rockwell © 1989, Cobblestone Publishing Inc., Peterborough, NH 03458. Reprinted by permission of the publisher. Illustration, "April Fool: Checkers" printed by permission of the Norman Rockwell Family Trust. Copyright © 1943 the Norman Rockwell Family Trust.

"The Smallest Show on Earth" reprinted from the July 1990 issue of *Ranger Rick* magazine, with permission of the publisher, the National Wildlife Federation. Copyright © 1990 by the National Wildlife Federation. Photograph reprinted by permission. Photo copyright © Nicole Duplaix/Peter Arnold, Inc.

"Patolli: A Game of Ancient Mexico" from *Faces*'s June 1990 issue: Ancient Mexico © 1990, Cobblestone Publishing Inc., Peterborough, NH 03458. Reprinted by permission of the publisher.

"When Does the 21st Century Begin?" from *Current Science*, November 17, 1989. Special permission granted by *Current Science* Magazine published by Field Publications. Copyright © 1989 by Field Publications.

"The Enigma of Time" from the March 1990 issue of *National Geographic* magazine. Excerpted by permission of the author. Copyright © 1990 by John Boslough.

"Half Past June" first appeared in *Cricket* magazine in April 1990. Copyright © by Arnold Spilka. Reprinted by permission of Marian Reiner for the author.

"Ctesibius" from *Classical Calliope*'s September 1989 issue: Ancient Inventions © 1989, Cobblestone Publishing Inc., Peterborough, NH 03458. Reprinted by permission of the publisher.

"Futuristic Frocks" from *Career World*, January 1990. Special permission granted by *Career World* Magazine published by Field Publications. Copyright © 1990 by Field Publications.

"China's Troubled Animals" from the January–February 1990 issue of *International Wildlife*. Reprinted by permission. Text copyright © 1990 by the National Wildlife Federation. Map by Tibor G. Toth. Reprinted by permission of the artist. Copyright © 1990 by Tibor G. Toth. Animal portraits reprinted by permission of the artist. Copyright © 1990 by Richard Orr.

"The Black Rhino" photograph from the January–February 1990 issue of *International Wildlife*. Reprinted by permission. Text copyright © 1990 by the National Wildlife Federation. Photo copyright © 1990 by Anthony Bannister.

"Going On-Line Worldwide" from *Career World*, March 1990. Special permission granted by *Career World* Magazine published by Field Publications. Copyright © 1990 by Field Publications.

"Computer 'Superhighway' to Link Nation's Computers" from *Current Science*, November 17, 1989. Special permission granted by *Current Science* Magazine published by Field Publications. Copyright © 1989 by Field Publications.

"There's No Place Like Home" from *Career World*, January 1990. Special permission granted by *Career World* Magazine published by Field Publications. Copyright © 1990 by Field Publications.

"Movies that Move Products" by Scholastic, Inc. *Choices* Magazine, January 1990. Reprinted by permission of Scholastic, Inc., NY.

"Harvest Celebration" from *Cobblestone*'s November 1989 issue: Pilgrims to a New World © 1989, Cobblestone Publishing Inc., Peterborough, NH 03458. Reprinted by permission of the publisher. Illustration, an 1894 calendar image entitled "The Return of the Mayflower," courtesy of The New England, Boston, MA.

"The Magician" reprinted by permission of Macmillan Publishing Company from *The Magician* by Uri Shulevitz. Copyright © 1973 by Uri Shulevitz. (Appeared in *Cricket* magazine, April 1990.)

"A Short History of Fireworks" from *Faces*'s February 1990 issue: Fire © 1990, Cobblestone Publishing Inc., Peterborough, NH 03458. Reprinted by permission of the publisher.

"Children in Art" first appeared in *Cricket* magazine in June 1990. Reprinted by permission of the author. Copyright ©1990 by Marjorie Jackson. *Tutankhamen Hunting* courtesy of the Egyptian Museum, Cairo. *Portrait of an Etruscan Boy*, *Children's Games*, and *The Maids of Honor* courtesy of SCALA/Art Resource, NY. *The Crossing of the Red Sea* courtesy of Klosterneuburg Abbey, Austria. *Prince Shōtoku as the Buddhist Saint Jizō* courtesy of the Freer Gallery of Art, Smithsonian Institution, Washington, D.C. [62.13 – Japanese painting: "Portrait of Prince Shotoku (aged 14) as the Bodhisattva Jizo"; Yamatoe school, Muromachi period (Ashikaga) (1334–1573), late 14th century; ink and color on silk: 49 1/8 × 27 1/8″ (124.7 × 68.9 cm.)]. *Self-portrait* of Albrecht Dürer courtesy Graphische Sammlung Albertina, Vienna. *A Sunday Afternoon on the Island of La Grande Jatte* courtesy the Art Institute of Chicago, Helen Birch Bartlett Memorial Collection © 1991 Art Institute of Chicago. *The New School* courtesy of Ministry of Education, Mexico City. *The Family* courtesy of Artists Rights Society © 1991 ARS NY/ADAGP.

"Yani" reprinted from the July 1990 issue of *Ranger Rick* magazine, with permission of the publisher, the National Wildlife Federation. Copyright © 1990 by the National Wildlife Federation. Photograph reprinted by permission. Photo copyright © 1990 by Chick Harrity.

"Children, Children Everywhere," which appeared in *Sesame Street* magazine, June 1990, is from *The Random House Book of Poetry for Children* by Jack Prelutsky, illustrated by Arnold Lobel. Copyright © 1983 by Random House, Inc. Reprinted by permission of Random House, Inc.

Garden silhouette by Pamela R. Levy first appeared in *Cricket* magazine in June 1990. Reprinted by permission of the artist. Copyright © 1990 by Pamela R. Levy.

"Hinamatsuri, The Japanese Festival of Dolls" from the March/April 1990 *Humpty Dumpty's Magazine*, copyright © 1990 by Children's Better Health Institute, Benjamin Franklin Literary & Medical Society, Indianapolis, Indiana. Used by permission of the author. Copyright © 1990 by Elinor Tropato Massoglia.

"Rumer Godden's Dolls" reprinted by permission of *Cricket* magazine, December 1989, Volume 17, No. 4.

"Calling All Brollies" from the April 1990 issue of *Highlights for Children*. Copyright © 1990 by Highlights for Children, Columbus, Ohio.